Sleeping with
One Eye Open

Sleeping with One Eye Open

My memoirs of childhood abandonment and emotional neglect

HELEN CONEYWORTH-SMITH

THE CHOIR PRESS

First published in the United Kingdom in 2021 by
The Choir Press

SBN 978-1-78963-195-1

Acknowledgments

To my childhood friends from Belvedere Road – Julie, Alison and Suzanne – who have always listened, supported and respected me, for the past forty-five years. I admire and love you all.

To the supportive teachers at Hessle C of E Junior School for all your patience, encouragement and positivity, therefore making my education and school days enjoyable. Special thanks to these amazing teachers – Mr Chignell (God rest his soul), Mrs Sellers and Mr Bury. Along with the best school friend anyone could wish for, Melanie.

Contents

CHAPTER 1

Conceive and Deceive

According to my mother I was a 'mistake' – not, as some parents may say 'a little surprise' or 'a gift from heaven/the stork/from God' (select as appropriate). No, apparently I was a bloody big mistake, an unwanted and unplanned baby. How I would hear this phrase throughout my life from my mother, who firstly obviously did not want a baby and, secondly, if she had to have a baby she wanted a boy first to name him Graham. Never mind, instead she got me – a baby girl she named Helen. I suppose I should be grateful, as I could have been called a lot worse.

It wasn't my fault she got pregnant and didn't take any reliable contraceptives, but she certainly blamed me for her becoming pregnant and ruining her career in 1964. Yes, her great professional 'career' (I'll use that word loosely): she used to work behind the counter at Skeltons bakery in Hessle Square! Not that I am knocking anyone working in a bakery, I certainly am not, but let's be honest, it wasn't as if she was a bank manager, headteacher or someone with some great authority in their job, as she made out. She sold sausage rolls, baps and crème puffs, for goodness sake.

She would often tell me how she loved her job. She had met my father there at Skeltons, when he used to come into the shop to buy his sandwiches or snacks at lunchtimes. He also used to work in Hessle at the General Post Office (GPO as it was called in those days) as a telegram boy and then progressed to a postman. So if they were so happy together, how did I spoil this idyllic life they had? I thought children could strengthen a relationship, not tear it apart?

As you can tell from these few paragraphs, my whole life would be a challenge and I had to prove and defend myself for being born and even existing.

Chapter 2

Neglect and Reject

We lived in a two-up, two-down terrace house in Salisbury Street in Hessle. I hated that house – it had a cold veranda with a corrugated plastic roof for the downstairs bathroom area and a small grassed back garden. I knew how small the grassed area was, as when I flew my paper aeroplanes over the grass they used to fly into next door's garden and I had to knock on the neighbour's door to retrieve them. She politely said not to knock anymore and just go and get it from her garden – she was probably fed up of my constant knocking!

There was hardly anywhere to kick a ball or do anything exciting outside. I remember a bit of grass where I just used to sit and pick daisies in the spring and summer, and when really bored I used to sit and look in the grass for four-leaf clovers. Something to do, I suppose, when you are totally fed up, with no mental stimulation, and you have to find things to do yourself.

My mother was always cleaning the house windows. She used a glass bottle of pink-coloured 'Windolene'. It contained a thick pink liquid that you had to smear on to the windows with a rag, then polish off again with a clean duster, or newspaper. I used to think it was a waste of time, as she would tell my father off for leaving fingerprints on the glass window or glass door, so why bother even cleaning them? I couldn't really care less if she cleaned, or didn't clean. I used to watch her and think to myself, 'is that what life is all about

– cleaning windows and door steps and doing washing in a twin tub every Monday and then huffing and puffing all day about it?' I was scared that this would be my future also, but also determined it wouldn't be.

Believe it or not, I was quite intelligent and I had found out how to be inquisitive and question everything. My father had taught me how to read – admittedly only newspapers, as I used to sit on his knee when he came home from work as he read the local newspaper. He had to entertain me whilst Mother was making the tea. So I learned to read newspapers really early in my life and I was bored even then, as I did not know what all the words meant, but I could read many sentences without pausing. My mother didn't have time to show me how to read or write, as she was always doing housework and doing irrational things like scrubbing the front doorstep and washing the walls. Watching her, I knew I never wanted to do such menial and monotonous tasks in my whole life. Unlike most other children, I actually looked forward to going to bed most nights just to go to sleep and break the monotony of the day.

It was October 1967, I was nearly four years old and it was cold in my bedroom – I remembered this fateful night, which would change my life, as if it were only yesterday.

I had been sent to bed early for no reason at all. When I was in bed trying to sleep, and for the next few hours, all I could hear was cat meowing noises from what seemed like outside in the back garden. I kept calling for my father, who was downstairs, asking him to come into my bedroom and listen to the cat. He came to the bottom of the stairs and told me to be quiet and get back into bed and get to sleep. After a while of hearing a manic cat screeching and meowing, I got fed up. I got out of bed again and noticed my parents' bedroom light was on, so walked across the small landing and into their large front bedroom. Their bedroom was normally out of bounds, and heaven help me if I entered the room, but sometimes at night I snuck in and lay in their double bed and sprawled out like a starfish, then my father had to carry me back into my own single bed. I loved their big bed and wished I could have one the same. As I approached their bedroom the meowing noise got louder and louder, and I suddenly realised that a cat must be in the bedroom – although we didn't have a cat, we had a dog! As I slowly opened the door and walked into the bedroom, I saw a wooden cot. Where that had appeared from I did not know. I walked over to it and saw a small baby in a pale blue fleecy BabyGro sort of outfit – it had a zip down the front of it and a blue silky ribbon tied to the top.

Yes, it was yet another 'mistake', this time named Matthew, my brother. His crying sounded like a cat meowing and the noise was ear piercing. My mother had had a home birth and didn't even tell me she was having a baby, if she did tell me it was kept 'quiet'. That was a shock, not a nice surprise. I didn't want to welcome a baby brother into my life; I was bored enough as it was.

A woman stranger was in the bedroom with my mother, the midwife. I was unsure about her and she gave me a small naked rubber doll as a 'treat'. I took it and went back into my small cold back bedroom – I would name the doll later on when I had time to think properly. I was still in shock. I remembered my mother saying to the midwife 'Oh she's very shy', which I wasn't – I just hated uncertainty, and definitely hated shocks. This was a bloody big shock!

I remember having a fluffy toy rabbit with a foot-long silky hair ribbon tied to its ear. I had tied it there. It was my comforter. I enjoyed weaving the silky ribbon between my fingers on my left hand, and then moving the soft ribbon over my top lip and under my nose, enjoying the comfort of the smoothness against my top lip. I don't remember having a dummy, just silky, smooth ribbons. Boy I needed that silky ribbon after seeing that baby creation in the next bedroom! I clung to my toy rabbit for dear life.

I had had a fairly reasonable (admittedly boring) life until Matthew came along. I used to be allowed an ice cream cornet with Kayli sprinkled on top (coloured, flavoured sugar crystals), from the newsagent at the top of the street on The Weir, and I loved this. Suddenly, a few months later, after HE had been born, I seemed to have been abandoned and left to my own ways, almost to fend for myself. No more ice cream cones with Kayli. All the attention went onto Matthew and I was jealous: he just seemed to have 'appeared' from nowhere, and no one thought to pre-warn me.

I suppose at least mother got the boy she wanted – although she always complained that she wanted a boy to be the eldest, and name him Graham, and a girl the youngest. Bloody hell, we had no chance in life to begin with did we really? Firstly we were mistakes and then we couldn't even be born in the right order! It was going to be an uphill struggle for us both . . .

We had a family dog that I loved, a miniature Yorkshire terrier called Mitzi. I wasn't sure where she was, as I enjoyed putting her in my doll's pram and pushing her gently around the small front room. Over the next few days I kept asking people where Mitzi was. I missed her. No one would answer me. We seemed to have numerous visitors since Matthew was born, which scared me as I had to sit by myself whilst they fussed around. They were probably midwives and doctors as it was a home birth, I was only guessing. I hated it and wanted privacy.

Unbeknown to me, until later on, Mother had said she

herself was ill and couldn't cope with two children AND a dog, and had given Mitzi away to my grandma (her Mother) permanently. This was the first time of many that my mother would get rid of things and upset me (and, later on, upset Matthew). She said that Mitzi was also ill. I did not think this was true. I wished Matthew would go away and then Mitzi might come back. I would see about getting rid of Matthew, then I would have my best friend, Mitzi, back. After all, my mother seemed to cope better before he arrived on the scene.

I picked up the doll the midwife had given me, and named it Lillian. The doll was quite chunky and pink coloured and had her hair up in a bun. Well, she didn't have real hair, it was just painted on. I think my mother had bought the doll but asked the midwife to give it to me as she was too ill to move out of the bed. My mother tried to make me change the name Lillian to something else, but I wouldn't. She kept asking where I got the name from, was it from my grandma or nana talking? I honestly didn't know. Maybe I had heard it on the television or heard someone say it in the street, who knows? Even at my young age I was annoyed at my mother for trying to get me to change the name of my doll. It was like she wanted to be in control of me, and I resented that.

CHAPTER 3

Educate and Communicate

I was four and a half years old and it was the summer of 1968. I remember that I was downstairs in the house, my mother said she was going upstairs and told me to keep out of the way as she was going to do some decorating in the back bedroom, my bedroom. She left Matthew, clipped to his harness, in his big Silver Cross coach pram in the small square hallway downstairs and I was left in the living room, being bored as usual. I must have wandered into the garden also, as I remembered it was chilly that morning, but what the hell do you do when you're by yourself? I didn't even have Mitzi, the dog, to talk to or play with anymore.

I came back into the living room, then I heard my mother run out of the bedroom. I was frightened at the stomping and running noises upstairs, but also needed to know what was going on. So I peered up the stairs from the small hallway to see my mother running quickly down the stairs, nearly knocking over the pram with Matthew in it, and running to the house phone in the hallway, nearly knocking me over also in the panic.

My mother had used a blowtorch to melt and remove the gloss paint on the skirting boards in the bedroom, but unfortunately, when she poured even more paraffin into the blowtorch, it had ignited again straight away and had literally set itself on fire. Then she dropped it onto the floor. The blowtorch was so well alight it then set the bedroom on fire as it was on the floor burning the bare floorboards, and she could not stop it. We had no upstairs bathroom for any water to extinguish the fire, so she had no option but to leave it burning and call the fire brigade. Hence, the panic of her running down the stairs to dial 999 from the telephone.

It was like being on a television comedy show, Mother pushing the pram into the small street with one hand, and then me being yanked by my hand into the street also. By this time, with all the shouting, screaming and crying from Mother, an audience had gathered outside. The bloody nosey neighbours. I hated this, why were we on show to the whole street? I just wanted to hide away and forget it all. Of course the fire brigade came (thankfully!) but the sirens caused even more people to flock around to see the drama. I remember the hoses being dragged inside the house and up the stairs. Then it seemed to be over with. After all, the neighbours couldn't see anything as the fire was in the back bedroom, so the crowd dispersed and we were allowed back in the house.

Seeing the firemen, who seemed so big and official and now in the house, I felt intimidated and hid behind the settee that was almost pushed up against the wall. 'Come on out!' Mother was shouting, and then the firemen were trying to persuade me to come out. They meant well, but it made me even more scared. Mother was having a cup of tea, or coffee, in one of her best china cups, as I remember a cup and saucer chinking together. I cannot remember how long I was behind that settee, but I never wanted to come out. Or maybe I was waiting until my father came home, which would have been a long wait as he was rarely home early nowadays. Thinking back, I would have loved to be a fly on the wall when my father did get home – I could imagine him being annoyed about the fire in the first instance, but also about us, after all we were left unattended downstairs for hours whilst Mother was doing the decorating. I suppose to us at the time this was normal, so thought nothing of it. I was now used to my own company anyway.

The fire drama really affected me as I felt scared, unprotected and unloved. No one had ever asked me how I was afterwards, plus I had to sleep in the upstairs bedroom, which still smelled of smoke. God knows how I went to sleep. In fact, I don't think I went to sleep for nights after that. I needed reassurance that this would not happen again, but I didn't get any.

During this year, I also found out that people aren't what they seem, and would lie to you to get their own way or cause you distress. I realised that I could trust no one. I was allowed out into the side street (Gladstone Street) to play and just wander around, but wasn't allowed to wander far. It was quieter than Salisbury Street, with not as many parked cars and people. Down this small street lived a few children my age, four to five years old. I remember Keith, who lived across the road. I think we became friends initially as both our mothers knew each other from school, but I never really knew. Maybe his mother just found me wandering the street and felt sorry for me and took me in, who knows?

Keith's house was bigger than ours, and he had a large concrete backyard where his mother let us both play; she would sit outside on a chair and watch us. His mother was tall and slim and she even allowed me to play with Keith's Action Men and toys. She was so nice to me that I felt overwhelmed and didn't know how to react. I wasn't used to being allowed to talk and play without being told to 'shut up' and 'sit down' – almost like how you would treat an untrained dog. My mother certainly wouldn't be sat outside with me playing. She just let me roam around the garden alone. Keith was a nice friend but I also didn't know how to play games with him – after all, he was a boy! It was all new to me but I knew I could trust him and his mother.

On the other side of the road was the future school bully – although obviously I did not know this at the time. I do not even think she lived down Gladstone Street, she just used to wander the streets of Hessle, looking to cause trouble. She was called Joanne and was taller than me, wider than me and had thick, black, wavy hair. One day she was out in the street. I had seen her before but managed to walk back to our back garden down the side snicket before she could talk to me. Today, unfortunately, I could not avoid her. She asked if I wanted a surprise, and if I did then I had to close my eyes and hold out my hands. I was obviously wary of this action, but also wary of what might happen if I did not follow her demands.

I did as she asked, or, rather, told me to do. Unknown to me she had some rose thorns in her hand, that she probably pinched from someone's prize roses in their front garden. My arms were outstretched with the palms of my hands pointing upwards. She then stabbed and scratched the rose thorns into my palms, obviously causing pain and them to bleed. I remember quickly opening my eyes and she was laughing at me. I ran home down the snicket to our back door and cried to my mother. I cannot remember her reaction, I think she helped me wash my hands, but I knew then who I could trust and who I couldn't. At least boys, such as Keith, weren't hurtful and vindictive like that to me. I knew, after that, that I would be wary of girls and stick with boys instead. Yeah boys could be violent and horrible also, but girls ... they seemed ten times worse.

To add to the trauma of this year, this was also the year I would start school. This was a shock to my system, after all I had been used to mainly being alone (I couldn't count

Matthew as he was only a baby). On my first day at school, I had a green pleated skirt and white blouse to put on. My mother walked me to school and she seemed excited to hand me over to any random teacher there, so she could go home and have some peace and quiet. I was very cautious about starting school.

We went through the doors at the front of the building and into a corridor area – the noise, hustle and bustle, smells of those black rubbery plimsolls, smells of different children, cabbage-like smells of school dinners being cooked was overwhelming. I needed time to adjust to this almost circus-like performance that was happening in front on me. I almost felt claustrophobic, even though it wasn't a confined space; it was just the sudden amount of people and noise in one area.

I just watched in amazement as people came and went, put their coats on the hooks in the corridor, and were then herded into a classroom, a bit like cattle. My mother had taken me to school the first time and I hadn't a clue how to get there or even get home again. Was she even collecting me? If so, what time was she collecting me? If not, how do I find my way back home? As we had gone through a snicket to get to the school, near the Hourne, I had lost my bearings, yet it was probably less than a mile from where we lived. I hated the unknown and I didn't dare ask anyone.

In the school corridor there was one child who didn't want to leave her mother. She was clinging to her mother's hand like it was life or death. Then an adult came along (presumably the teacher) and took hold of the child's other hand and tried to encourage, or more likely force her to come away from her mother and go into the classroom. It was like watching a tug-of-war. Child in the middle, now crying hysterically, her arms outstretched, and both adults pulling her in their own different directions. A bit like pulling a Christmas cracker, was she going to split in half or just explode? The child eventually made it into the classroom with a tear-stained face. Later I got to know her as Melanie. She was now my friend. She was the total opposite to me in many ways, she seemed to be a mummy's girl and very needy and fussy about everything, but we got on well and she was kind to me. 'Opposites attract', as the saying goes.

Hessle Church of England Infants' School was the school name, and I did grow to love it. It was daunting entering a classroom with another twenty-five children or so in it, all on their first day, but some had older siblings so they knew what to expect and how to talk and behave. I hadn't a clue. On a positive note, I had to think that this was away from the cold house in Salisbury Street with a freezing bathroom, and I could learn to talk to other children. I didn't have much in the way of communication skills, as I hadn't really met many other children. In addition I was always told to 'shut up – I've got a headache' or 'be quiet, you're getting on my nerves' at home, so talking hadn't exactly been encouraged. I don't think there was such a thing as a children's nursery in those days, and if there was, I certainly wasn't allowed there to play or learn as it would have cost money.

The furthest I had actually been in my life so far was to my grandma's house near Hessle Square. I knew I had also been to my nana's house in Hull a few times, but couldn't really tell how far it was from Hessle. My grandma looked after me now and again, and that was about it. I hadn't ventured far in my four, nearly five, years of life. I had led a sheltered life, so to go to school was a big shock for me.

My mother didn't have anyone to visit the house as she was a bit of a loner. Unfortunately, this had rubbed off onto myself and therefore my skills were only in reading and doing craft things with my hands or playing with my Fuzzy Felt animals. My mother's tone was always of frustration and anger, and I knew I could hear myself speaking in the same way, but couldn't help it as I didn't know how to present myself in any other way. I would snap at other people with responses such as 'yes' or 'no', or not talk at all, there was no happy medium. I think the years of being told 'for goodness sake – BE QUIET' and that I 'shouldn't even be seen, never mind heard', had made me almost deliberately mute and voiceless with no opinion, not 'shy' as people would call me. I was never shy; I had plenty to say but I was restricted by Mother in what I could say, but no one realised that. I had to say my opinions in my head, just like thoughts, and keep them to myself. Because I wasn't allowed to talk at home, I was very observant as to what was happening around me, especially to sounds and smells, and this frustrated my mother even more as she thought I was always being nosey.

Nowadays I would have probably been on the special educational needs register at school with 'social, emotional and mental health' issues, but then any SEN co-ordinator would have been shocked that I could read a newspaper fluently and read confidently out loud. It was just my own words I had difficulty communicating or saying. Little did the school realise that in the near future my brother would have the same issues.

I loved reading at school as it came naturally and easily and there were loads of different books to read, after all I had been reading the local newspapers and smutty Sunday newspapers at my nana's house in Hull for about a year! Did I really need to learn the flipping alphabet when I could repeat it backwards, never mind forwards? Why did I need to know that A is for Apple and B is for Ball, etc.? This was totally boring to me. In the Sunday newspapers B would be for Breasts and Bottom! I used to giggle to myself about this but knew if I mentioned this to the teacher then I would get told off.

Maths, however, was literally another story. I hated maths and could not really understand it, as it wasn't really logical in my mind. I was frustrated with this, as other children seemed to understand it more than myself, but I had never been taught maths by my father – he hadn't a clue, so I was way out of my depth. I could do simple arithmetic but used to memorise a lot of it as I could not work it out in my head. Also I used to think it was boring, and why would I want to know how to add 1 + 2 together? Maths was, unfortunately, my weakness, and still is.

After school, my mother did collect me at the school gates. I knew never to show any enthusiasm about school as my mother always said she had a headache or was tired from looking after Matthew. So I was just quiet and trotted alongside her like a well-trained dog, on the way home.

When I got home I missed my dog, Mitzi, like mad and cried for her all the time. My life had been turned upside down with losing Mitzi and gaining a screaming baby brother. My mother thought I would miraculously be different when I started school, and I remember her telling my aunty, 'Oh Helen is going to school soon, so she'll get better' like I had some kind of illness or disease! I felt like I was being 'farmed out' like an animal in a field, and after the first days at school I certainly thought that.

I remember my mother telling people that she had given up work before I was born, so I could not really understand why she was always stressed. After all, my father used to come home tired out from his nine hour, or more, shift at work. I liked it best when, on occasions, he was home early by 5pm as I liked to sit on his left knee, as he sat and read the local newspaper, whilst my mother prepared the tea. He used to read the words out to me and ask my opinion, and I used to try and follow his words in the text. He was quite methodical and used to explain what some of the words meant, as obviously I hadn't much of a clue about the long words, but to me it was new and interesting and I thrived on it. Sometimes I needed a bit of structure and organisation rather than doing my own thing. I was a bored child and sometimes found it hard to make my own entertainment with the lack of interesting resources and toys.

I always hated flowers, and still do. I don't know why, maybe it is because they just wilt and die after a few days and seem to be a waste of money and effort. Maybe it is the smell of them that puts me off, as some of the scents are either too strong or cause headaches. I just don't know.

My mother used to buy flowers and pussy willows for flower displays in her one and only vase. I used to think it was a waste of time buying flowers and to create such arrangements, but used to watch her put the flowers into a vase and attempt to arrange them in some sort of order. What order should these be in? I could never understand, and I don't think she did either. They just looked randomly thrown into a vase; I could do better myself. Or better still, don't bother at all.

The worse thing that can happen to me is that I become bored, as I just do things that no one else would even dream of. So, yes, I became bored sat in the house, with only a few toys to play with and a flower display to look at. I was also limited to when I could watch the black and white television. There was probably not a lot on the television in those days anyway, in the late 1960s, but it was a welcome distraction. As mentioned previously, I loved putting and holding silky ribbons near my top lip as a comforter. When stroking the pussy willows in the vase they felt quite silky and velvet like, similar to my ribbon. The pussy willows came on a small branch and each one was the size of a small salted peanut, but they were all quite furry and smooth like a silky peanut. I pulled a pussy willow off the small branch and held it in my right hand and placed it on my top lip to feel the texture, it felt lovely and smooth. Unfortunately I managed to inhale at that precise time and the pussy willow was sniffed up and then stuck inside my nose, no matter how much I tried to blow my nose on my knitted cardigan sleeve, it just seemed to be stuck.

I was dreading telling my mother that I had a pussy willow stuck up the inside of my nose, but I had to brave it and tell her. I had a story in my head that I would blame Matthew, and say that he had shoved it up my nose. Unfortunately the story wasn't believable as he was only about one year old, still in his Silver Cross pram and probably not even walking. I found Mother and told her. She wasn't happy and I remember being frog-marched to the doctor's house down Chestnut Avenue in Hessle, an old Georgian or Victorian property. I think his name was Doctor Cameron, but I could be wrong. Matthew was being pushed in his pram, and Mother was walking like she was on a mission. It wasn't far to walk, not even five minutes, but you would have thought it was a trek to the other side of Hessle the way she was huffing and puffing. To be honest I cannot remember much about the treatment I got there, only the large overpowering house that had a downstairs room as a doctor's surgery used for out-of-hours and emergency appointments. It also was quite dark and cold and smelled a bit fusty. Apparently the doctor got a large pair of tweezers and managed to remove the offending pussy willow. It couldn't have been that painful as I am sure I would have remembered it! I made a mental note to myself never to try that again.

The kitchen at Salisbury Street was small, dark and cold and led to an even colder veranda that had a roof made out of flimsy corrugated plastic. In the kitchen we had a gas cooker with an oven that needed a flame to ignite it. This was a proper 1960s-style oven and to light it you had to turn on the gas by a knob above the oven door. Then there was a type of metal and plastic-handled wand, attached by a hook to the right side of the oven, you had to press the plunger on the wand downwards and it released gas to the end of the wand. The wand then had to be put into the flame called the pilot light, which was constantly lit in the centre of the hobs. So in effect you had to light the wand with a naked flame, then put the lit wand into the open oven, where there was a gas outlet to light the actual oven. It must have been easier, and safer, to surely get an electric cooker like my grandma had? If the pilot light went out on the hobs, which it did sometimes if it was draughty, then there was a smell of escaping gas lingering through the kitchen.

I had an idea in my head that I would try and gas Matthew out. I had heard that people could die from gas leaks, so this seemed like a good idea. My theory was that I would kill him then I could get my dog Mitzi back, after all my mother could cope with me and the dog before he was born, so it was only him putting a spanner in the works and stopping me getting Mitzi.

I remember walking into the kitchen, Matthew was sat upright, clipped to his harness in his Silver Cross coach pram which was near the oven. My mother was upstairs and had left me for what seemed like ages. I tried to move the pram nearer the cooker but couldn't seem to push it. The brake was probably on. However, the wand attached to the cooker would reach the pram, so it didn't really matter. By the time my mother had come downstairs and into the kitchen, she found the oven wand in Matthew's pram under the blankets. I had continuously pushed the plunger down on it to try and gas him out, and the kitchen smelled of gas. Luckily I didn't have the sense to actually ignite the wand, otherwise there would have been another house fire, and possibly a death to account for.

Unfortunately (or fortunately!) my plan backfired and Matthew was still alive. Obviously I was told off, but it was worth it. Anything to get Mitzi back home. In the future I would have to try a different tactic.

CHAPTER 4

Disown and Alone

I remember my mother being in bed for most of the time during the day and me having to then walk to school alone. I think she, or my father, must have woken me up each school day as I didn't have an alarm clock. I am not even sure if I had breakfast or how I got dressed but I just got on with it. After all, my father went out to work early at about 7am and there was no one to help me. I was tired out from Matthew continuously crying during the night, and no doubt Mother would have been too.

I memorised the route to school from the occasions Mother had taken me. Luckily I had a good memory, and also found a shortcut. I would go to the end of Salisbury Street, cross the road called Tower Hill, then walk alongside the lopsided wall at All Saint's church. There was a zebra crossing to cross the busy road, then walk down Swinegate until reaching the metal school gates at the back of the school. They led to the Hourne, and both the junior and infant schools. Then I had to walk across a wobbly paving slab path that led to the playground at the junior school, then walk amongst all the children at junior school that were playing ball or other games before school time, then walk across a car park to the infant school. If I was feeling brave I would take a shortcut and walk across both school fields, which were supposed to be out of bounds before and after school. If a junior school teacher saw this from the classroom then they would bang on the classroom window at you. Not that I cared – after all, how did they know who you are?

The worse thing about walking across the school field was that there was a separate school canteen that always seemed to have smells of cooked cabbage and boiled meat coming from it. To be honest it smelled like dog meat or some kind of fatty mince my grandma cooked in her kitchen for her dog (or was it my dog? I did not know anymore). It was never a nice smell of freshly cooked bread like at the local bakery, or chips. When my grandma made some chips with oil in her chip pan, they smelled and tasted delicious. The canteen smells were certainly something I wanted to forget, as they made me feel queasy, although unfortunately I had to stay for school dinners. The canteen was one building but split into two, one smaller side for the infants and the other for juniors. They had shared kitchens though, so they cooked the same food, but the smell just lingered for hours before and after dinnertime.

In those days no questions were asked as to how you got to school by yourself, or where your mother was. We just played in the playground before school began and waited until the bell rang. A teacher came out into the playground and actually rang a traditional school hand bell (like a town crier would use nowadays). I would make my way into the cloakroom and change into my black plimsolls (or sannies) and go into the classroom. To be honest, I thought it was the norm. It was only when I would see Melanie and her mother arriving at the school together hand in hand from the long walk down Swanland Road, then I couldn't work out if she was the normal one, or was I? If Melanie arrived in her mother's car I was in awe, as we never had a car; my father had a moped and that was it. We had to use a bus even to get to Nana's house in Hull.

Obviously as we didn't have a car. We didn't go out as a

family unless we walked, and the only place to walk was to Hessle Foreshore, which had Dunston's Shipyard and the railway line nearby, that was it. My father would take his camera to take photos of the trains at Hessle train station or from the footbridge, and also the ships being built at the shipyard. I was bored, my feet hurt from walking and I didn't want to be there. How I wished we had a car like Melanie's mother did. I bet they went to lots of different and nice places. I was very jealous.

I cannot even remember how I walked home again from school, if it was winter and dark I certainly wouldn't be walking across the school field as it was too scary. I am not sure if my mother collected me? I am sure if this was the case nowadays social services would be involved. But in those days, the school bell rang at the end of school time and all the children went to the cloakroom, changed from their plimsolls to their outside shoes, put on coats and ran outside into the playground. The teachers hadn't a clue if the parents were there or not.

Sometimes I had to go to my grandma's house after school. I didn't know why I had to go there, but I did as I was told. Maybe mother wanted a longer lie in bed, who knows? To be honest I was just an outsider now and Matthew took pride of place in the ranking order at home, so I just accepted this. My grandma's house was easier to walk to from school anyway as there was only one road to cross. My grandma was my mother's mother. I didn't have a grandad anymore as he had apparently died a few years earlier when I was just a baby. My grandad had been a skipper on the trawlers in Hull, or so I was told. So he was used to being away from home for months at a time as he was fishing in the North Atlantic. He would then come back home and 'splash the cash', and treat my grandma and all the family to expensive gifts, meals and clothes. The trawlermen were known as 'three day millionaires', getting paid a lot of money for being at sea, then coming home, spending their wages on their family before going back to sea a few days later. Some trawlermen spent their days off work drinking in the pubs down Hessle Road in Hull. I am not sure if my grandad did. I couldn't see my grandma allowing that.

I presume that is why my grandma didn't work, as she seemed quite wealthy compared to our family, and had a fairly large three-bedroomed semi-detached house in one of the closest streets to Hessle Square. My grandad's money from the trawlers would have paid for it no doubt and she didn't need to work.

When I used to go to my grandma's I could not understand why one of my cousins was always there. She was nearly a year younger than myself and was always the centre of attention and got everything she asked for, whereas I didn't seem to get a great deal of anything and had to make my own entertainment. I didn't realise at the time, but my mother's sister, who was ten years younger than my mother, had become pregnant at the age of fifteen and wanted to keep the baby. My mother, ever since then, always looked down on her sister, Linda, but seemed to adore Linda's daughter, who was 'born out of wedlock' as my mother used to say in her sarcastic tone.

Then, and even years later, I was always compared to my cousin Carol. 'Why can't you be more like Carol?' my mother used to say. 'She always says please and thank you, whereas you don't.' The difference was, in my opinion, that she was a spoilt child. She and her mother lived at my grandma's house, didn't have any stress or worry about money or work. Carol had loads of toys and even a wooden doll's house. I didn't really understand it. But then I overheard my mother talking to someone in Hessle Square whilst shopping. She said, 'Oh yes she kept the baby and the father was a married man!' Obviously this was relating to her sister and at the time I didn't really comprehend why there was no father on the scene, but now I knew. He was possibly married and may even have had other children! I reckon it was the scandal of Hessle, but in fairness to my Aunty Linda, she did keep the baby. I am sure many other expectant mothers-to-be would not have done. She had to live with the scandal of being a single mother, this was the 1960s where gossip was rife. I would have thought my mother would have defended Linda, after all she was her sister. But this didn't seem to be the case. It all seemed a bit strange to me, especially as my mother seemed to thrive on scandal and gossip about her own family, as long as it didn't involve herself.

Carol got everything. She even got a red coloured Fisher Price children's record player with big thick plastic colourful records to put on it. I was jealous. I bet she didn't have to make her own entertainment at home by picking daisies in the back garden like I did. She would wind this record player up that was placed on my grandma's expensive wooden sideboard, and then do a dance to the music with her mother and my grandma clapping at her and encouraging her. She loved the attention and lapped it up. It made me feel physically sick and I wanted my own space. This was like a nightmare. What was wrong with these people always wanting to be the centre of attention? I knew that when I played with Keith and his toys in his garden, he wouldn't have done such a thing as dancing around. So far I'd had bad experiences of friendships with girls, the big bully Joanne had stabbed me in the palm of my hand with rose thorns, and now I was subjected to the horror of a child dancing around the room whilst everyone else clapped and was being fake and happy. I knew that I wouldn't be playing with any girls again, except Melanie at school, of course – she seemed almost normal and certainly wasn't a show-off.

The child's record player was playing with the tinkling sound of music. I hid behind the large armchair that was nearby, so my grandma and aunty couldn't see me, and kept putting my hand up to the sideboard and pressing the button to stop the record player, to halt this almost circus-like performance. Of course I got told off, Carol began crying and I was pushed out of the main room through the kitchen with a sliding door and out into the back garden and called a 'horrible child' by my aunty. Not that I cared. Why should I? I had peace and quiet in the garden. The unfortunate thing is that my mother found out. She came to collect me from my grandma's house and was told about my bad behaviour.

I walked with my mother back to Salisbury Street in silence, my brother was in his pram. I could tell there was a bad atmosphere. When I got into the living room she turned on me and thought nothing of bending me over her knee and slapping my legs and backside until they were red raw with slap marks and it stung like mad. Then I was sent to my bedroom. I was in shock. Yes, I admit I was stupid and childish for doing such a silly thing at my grandma's house, but it was hardly an evil thing I had done, and did it warrant the pain I was feeling? I couldn't even sit down, so climbed into my bed still in my clothes and without any tea. I wasn't hungry anyway. This action from my mother sent questions through my head – were all children treated like this? Maybe they were but never told anyone? My mother had told me that children 'should be seen and not heard', did that mean that I could never talk again? My mind was working overtime. I decided in my own mind that I would not talk again or even act sociably, then that surely should stop any further slapping and hitting. I knew it would be hard not to talk in class at school, but I could not risk this torture and pain again.

For some reason at this age of five years, I remember going the first time to Hornsea on the east coast. I was with my grandma and aunty and they were looking at caravans for sale. Later on I was told by my mother (I am not sure if this was true or not) that my grandma had previously bought a static caravan at Hornsea to be used for my aunty to stay in and hide away whilst she was pregnant! I was not sure who, or what, to believe. My mother seemed to spread gossip and untruths wherever she went. It seemed to make her feel she had the upper hand, as she thought she was so perfect.

The static caravan sites at the north end of Hornsea were situated on the cliff tops overlooking the beach, with massive waves that sometimes came crashing to the bottom of the cliffs and even washed some of the cliffs away into the sea. The noise and spray from the waves was sometimes frightening. Hornsea also had amusement arcades. I loved those and had never seen them before; the penny machines were the best. There were also chip shops on the seafront, and shops that sold toffee apples, sticks of rock and candy floss during the summer months. To a child it was heaven compared to boring Hessle. Little did I know that later in life the caravan at Hornsea would almost become my second home.

CHAPTER 5

Reprimand and Demand

This was 1970 and we moved house. I wasn't sure why. I had overheard my mother once, telling someone that my father had gone out to work in the TV detector van and when he knocked on someone's door to question their TV licence, he had got beaten up. I do not know if this was true as she did sometimes make up elaborate stories. She even said that the assault made the local papers and they had put our address in it, hence the reason for moving. But who knows? I certainly will never know.

We moved from a two-bedroom terrace house to a three-bedroomed terrace house down Belvedere Road in Hessle, which was more near the border of Hull then the centre of Hessle. I originally wasn't really bothered about it, but realised it was quite isolated and further away from the shops or anywhere. There was nowhere to walk to, and I had no one to talk to. I had left Keith and his Action Men toys, and did not know anyone who lived down the road. Yes, the house was a lot bigger than Salisbury Street and I had a bigger bedroom, that hadn't been set on fire. Matthew had his own bedroom too but it was really a box room. You couldn't even fit anything else in there except a cot or single bed and a small chest of drawers. There was a very small bathroom with a bath, sink and toilet in it. It couldn't have been more than two metres square to walk into. Even the bathroom door had to be changed into a homemade sliding door as when it opened into the bathroom there was hardly any room to walk into it easily and close it behind you. I suppose it was a slight improvement on Salisbury Street.

I remember the next-door neighbour, to the right of our property, was a lady named Doreen, who lived with her elderly mother. Doreen was my mother's age, but kind to me, no shouting, and she used to give me chocolate treats and Jelly Tots that my parents would never do. She worked at Boots the chemist in Hessle and Hull and I really wanted to work there when I was older. She used to come home from work in her white tunic and looked really professional. I wasn't sure what she did at the chemist but she looked really cool and I wanted to be like her.

One advantage of moving to Belvedere Road was that school was a bit closer for me to walk to – only about 10 minutes, or about five if you ran. Our catchment area for primary schools was now Penshurst, but my mother wanted me to stay at All Saints C of E, so that was fine with me, as it was even closer then Penshurst. The only issue was that down Belvedere Road, all the other children of infant and junior school age went to Penshurst, so I felt like a bit of an outsider as they knew each other, but the close neighbours that had young children all made friends with me. We had a tenfoot to play in also, so that was a bit safer than playing at the front near the main road.

I hated staying for school dinners at infants as I hated the food; it was greasy, stodgy and inedible. These dinners actually put me off eating meat forever. I remember chunks of meat on the plate that you could not even chew and almost choked on, and had to spit it out on the side of your plate. Along with the smell of mint sauce this was disgusting and actually turns my stomach – even now. One of the dinner ladies told me off for spitting the meat out onto the side of my plate, I thought to myself that even my grandma's dog couldn't chew it – never mind a child! I would rather starve. I wasn't a fussy eater; I just couldn't chew lumps of gristle.

At dinnertime at the infant school you were lucky to have more than one choice of a meal, and if you were late for the dinner queue, for example if you had popped to the toilets, you were lucky to get anything at all except something like gravy and mash. Not that I minded that, at least I could swallow it without choking.

It was a strange routine for dinners. In the school canteen you all sat at tables that seated eight pupils each, and the person who was sat opposite you on the table had to also collect that person's meal. How bizarre. I think their theory was that it saved every child going up individually, therefore reducing the queue size by half and saving time. But who knew? I never understood the rules there. Sometimes you only got one meal choice, like it or lump it. None of the 'Have you any dietary requirements/dietary needs/food allergies?' questions you are asked nowadays. In the 1970s it was a case of 'eat it or leave it and starve'.

So it was my turn to stand in the dinner queue and collect my plate of food, and in addition, another plate for the person who sat opposite me. I had just got my two empty plates, one in each hand, and moved down the dinner queue, I cannot remember what food I had on my plate but at the end of the queue there was a dinner lady who had the gravy ladle and she just poured it over the top of the food on both plates. It was hard to balance a plate full of food in each hand, but I managed. In those days there was none of those proper food trays or containers that you now use to stop food sliding off!

As I moved away from the serving hatch to go back to my table, one of the teachers suddenly started shouting at another pupil for some reason. She was called Mrs Hall and, in my opinion, she was a loud, mouthy cow anyway and most of the children hated her. She was short and fat with brown wavy hair. She shouted at the child and bellowed out like the bloody foghorn on the River Humber, 'Everyone STOP – stand still.' You didn't argue with her, it was like a game of musical statues where you daren't move, but there was no music and no prize! To keep still was easier said than done when you have small hands, holding two large warm plates of food, and gravy almost dripping off the plates.

After about a minute of Mrs Hall shouting irrationally at the child, my hands and wrists were hurting by keeping still for so long and the gravy slowly began to slide off one of the plates. I was near another table but daren't put the plates down as I would have been told off for moving.

Unfortunately, the warm gravy slid off the plate right down another child's back who was sat waiting for his dinner. I remember it was a boy and he went mad by screaming and crying (not that I blamed him). It probably shocked him or even burned him. Mrs Hall stopped shouting at the original child and then began shouting at me for scalding someone. The whole canteen full of children and teachers turned and looked at me instead. I must have gone bright red with embarrassment but no one came to help me, so the food just slid off the plate, fell onto the floor, splattering everywhere, even onto my socks. I couldn't win; I had to stay still, as Mrs Hall was yelling like a deranged banshee, but in doing so the weight and warmth of the plates was too much for a small child. In those days there was no such thing as 'Health and Safety'! It certainly wouldn't be allowed nowadays. I daren't tell my mother as I would get a telling-off again, so just kept it to myself. I dreaded it in case the school rang my mother at home to tell her of the incident – luckily they didn't. I knew if she found out I would be getting some kind of punishment.

As we had just moved into the house, my mother again

decided to do all the decorating and painting herself, or with my father if he was home from work. Again, Matthew and I were left to make our own entertainment either downstairs or in the garden. Bearing in mind I was only six and Matthew was nearly three years old. Mother laid down the rules as usual, and we were not allowed to go into the front room, so my mother made my father put a lock on the top of the two sliding doors to this room so we couldn't reach it and open the doors. I didn't mind the front room as it was a lot warmer than the rest of the house as the sun came in through the windows, but apparently this had to be the 'best room' and no one was allowed in it except at Christmas time. God knows what that was all about? To this day I am still puzzled by it. Why have a room you are not allowed to go into?

My father liked the garden as it had a shed, where he could hide away and make out he was doing something con-structive, and we also had a garage that was falling down, which had an asbestos roof. In the house there was a loft space that my father eventually boarded out where he created his own model railway layout. All these places such as the shed, garage and loft, were where my father could sneak away from my mother and have his own peace and quiet. Unfortunately, Matthew and I didn't have that luxury and were usually within shouting or hitting distance of Mother at all times.

My mother had spent time glossing skirting boards upstairs, I cannot remember her using a blowtorch this time, so she must have been warned about it from my father, or maybe the bedroom catching fire at the other house had scared and mentally scarred her. She used to save her old jam jars, and put turpentine in them to rinse the paintbrushes out so she could use them again and again. In those days you had to leave paint brushes to soak in turpentine for a while before washing them and reusing them. The smell of turpentine is a strong chemical odour and not nice, especially when mixed with gloss paint, which in those days might have had lead in it. She would soak the used paint brushes in the jam jars in the shed until she needed them again.

It was a warm summer's day and Matthew had stripped off all his clothes (for some unknown reason) and was running around naked down the long narrow back garden. I went outside to the back garden and could see my mother talking over the small dividing fence to Doreen, our neighbour. Doreen and my mother were always talking over the fence to each other, I wasn't sure how my mother was friends with her, as Doreen was so nice, whereas my mother was the opposite. I'm not sure if they knew each other before we moved into the house, but my mother was always whinging to her about 'the kids' (meaning us) and what we had been up to that was naughty. I knew Doreen felt compassion towards Matthew and myself. My mother was talking for ages as usual, Matthew was now getting bored, I was also bored; Matthew was too young to have a conversation or to play games with. I walked down the garden path, past my mother and went to the bottom of the garden where the shed door had been left open.

The shed was kitted out with old-fashioned light blue hand-painted kitchen units and there were loads of empty jam jars, some with dead spiders in or cobwebs. In one of the jam jars I saw that there was the paintbrush that had been used for painting the white gloss onto the skirting boards, and was now in the jam jar with its bristles soaking in turpentine. I reached over to the paintbrush and took it out of the jar. It was dripping white gloss paint and turps. I asked Matthew to come into the shed and stand still, which he obligingly did, then I painted his willy using the paintbrush. I thought it looked quite good to be honest, it was white gloss and stood out against his slightly tanned skin. I was jealous that I didn't have such an appendage to decorate. If I could have found some glitter then it would have looked even better, but the only glitter I had previously used was unfortunately still at school for Christmas decorations. I must admit that the turps and white gloss were now dripping off his willy.

Matthew turned and ran out of the shed and to my mother who was still talking. I remember her saying, 'Oh Doreen I'll have to go, the kids are being naughty again!' Then she takes Matthew's arm and drags him up the garden path to the house, presumably to scrub or wash his willy. I remember being told off afterwards and Matthew was then dressed and upset. My mother blamed me for 'attention seeking'. Well I wasn't, I was just bored, I had no proper outside toys and was just expected to make my own entertainment. We were both left to our own ways whilst she was always painting skirting boards or attempting to wallpaper, or just spent all the time cleaning up. Alternatively her other new pastime was now talking to Doreen over the fence for hours on end. I used to think, 'Why have children if you aren't going to look after them, or even want to be with them?' I was more upset that other children in my class at school went with their parents to parks or toy shops to buy nice crayons and pencils. We never went anywhere. No wonder I was bored. I was either looking at four walls in the house, or a boring garden each day.

My mother had constant fits of rage. She even shouted at us both one day that 'I never wanted children – you were both mistakes, you should never have been born.' Matthew didn't really understand, after all he was only three years old, but I knew we were going to be fending for ourselves after that outburst. I got it. She was so mentally hurtful, but I was clever and tried to be about ten steps ahead of her, and knew never to show emotional hurt as she enjoyed that. She actually enjoyed seeing me cry. I used to hold my head up high and just stare at her, and that annoyed her even more. I realised that when she physically hurt me by hitting me, that if I shouted and cried even louder the neighbours could hear, so she might stop hitting or hurting me sooner. I knew how to play her mind games even at this early age.

CHAPTER 6

Blameful and Shameful

Yet again, I remember Mother spending most of her time in her bed, and Matthew and I just doing our own 'thing' such as playing, arguing or anything else really. I managed once to speak to my father when he was alone and told him that I found it hard to do anything right without being told off or hit by Mother, as well as look after Matthew. I was seven years old for goodness sake. He just told me it was my mother's 'nerves' affecting her, but she needed bedrest and would get better. In other words she could not cope and we had to take the brunt of it. I am not sure if she was bipolar, depressed, had underlying mental problems, who knew? To be told she just had 'nerve' problems was an insult to my intelligence. I knew Mother had mental problems and no one was helping her – or us! If my father could not help me, then no one could. Not that he knew what she was like to me, as he was at work most of the time, deliberately keeping out of her way.

My father sometimes had the backlash of her moods when he returned home from work at his usual time past 7pm. My mother was always the one to say to us 'wait until I tell your father when he gets home!' if we had been 'naughty'. So Matthew and I used to hope he would get home late, past 8pm, when we were in bed so he wouldn't give us a second telling-off! I knew that he didn't like telling us off, but felt he had to do it as Mother had saved all her anger up for when he got home, and demanded he also hit us (which he rarely did), or shout and punish us (which he did regularly – on her command). He was too weak to be a father sometimes and that upset me. Even he was sometimes confused as to what we had done that was so wrong, but because Mother was screaming and screeching like someone possessed by the devil, he had to go ahead and discipline us to keep her quiet. Our feelings, or telling him that we hadn't done anything wrong, were ignored. In fact it encouraged Mother even more by her saying to my father, 'Look that's what they are like – always answering back, being rude and cheeky!' I really hated my father sometimes, as he was not being fair or understanding.

On the 20th January in this year (1971), postal workers went on strike for the first time ever. So my father, along with other post office employees, were suddenly on strike. There was hardly any money coming into our house, according to Mother. The strike only lasted for seven weeks and finished in March, but obviously at the time no one knew when it would finish. They were striking about a low pay rise, so ironically they weren't getting paid whilst on strike, but in the long term there would hopefully be an increased salary. I remember seeing something on the television about the postal strike. My father was at home more, and that encouraged her to shout at him even more, that there was not enough food in the house to feed us. Seemingly, it was his fault that we had moved house to Belvedere Road and now could not afford the mortgage. I was surprised he didn't walk out to be honest. I think he would have done, but he had nowhere to go as he didn't get along too well with his parents. Now my mother was even more stressed and I could see the signs that I would bear the brunt of this. I had nowhere to go either, she was a bloody volcano waiting to erupt, or a bloody ticking time-bomb.

Her meltdowns and verbal explosions were continual, even after my father went back to work in March. There was no excuse. If she was that worried about money then surely she could have got a job for a few weeks and my father could have looked after us at home? After all she used to say that Matthew and I made her give up her career at Skeltons bakery. Why didn't she ask for a part time or temporary job there then? I sometimes felt sorry for my father, he worked long hours and travelled back and forwards to work on his moped in rain and snow, or whatever the weather, and this is how she treats him! God I hated her at times. I was hoping things would be better when my father went back to work and she had his money again, but it wasn't.

Although I hated Matthew, I had to try and look after him as he could not talk (due to us always being told to shut up) so I had to try and ask for things on his behalf. He was scared of talking as he'd seen the way I had been treated, so he didn't even attempt to talk. He could talk, however, but rarely out loud, and did whisper to me sometimes. I remember his big blue eyes looking at me, and as much as I disliked him for being Mother's favourite child, I knew I had to save him and take punishment for whatever he needed. He looked so innocent and small compared to me. How could I let him starve or be punished like I was? He was now almost four years old for God's sake and didn't know any different. No wonder he was always walking around the house and back garden half naked, as he didn't know how to dress himself, or even able to get his clothes out of the one chest of drawers he had in his small box room they called a third bedroom.

The wooden chest of drawers were really old and heavy, so it was hard for even me to pull the drawers open. Once, without thinking properly, I opened all the drawers together looking for some clothes for him, and the whole chest of drawers nearly fell over onto me. Again I had no one to help, I daren't cry out as I would be punished if Mother heard me, I just had to try and push one drawer in at a time and see if it would balance back so I wasn't crushed. That was our daily life in the house, to see if we could survive each day. We both knew that we would be hit on a daily basis but not sure when, and why, and now the apprehension of the 'not knowing' was affecting us both with anxiety and stress issues. We both cried a lot, and that was even before the hard-core mental and physical abuse even started.

Matthew's bedroom had a wall decorated with teddy bear wallpaper. The teddy bears weren't cute ones, they were like Steiff bears with unusual triangular faces, strange shaped nostrils and big black eyes. The wallpaper had the bears comically drawn in different situations, e.g. having a picnic and rowing a boat. Matthew had wanted car or train wallpaper, but wasn't allowed that. Mother chose the wallpaper from a shop down Hull Road in Hessle, and decided that the wall nearest his bed would have the new wallpaper on it. This was okay until the next morning when my mother went into his bedroom.

Matthew said he was frightened as the bears were watching him sleep and they had big black eyes with no eyelids. Being scared, he had licked his finger over and over again and rubbed away all the teddy bear eyes that he could reach. There were tiny bits of wallpaper all over his bedding. I thought it was hilarious but obviously my mother didn't. I think my mother painted over the wallpaper after that instead. If he had got car or train wallpaper this wouldn't have happened. I kept this to myself but was secretly laughing to myself. She always thought she knew best.

Apparently my mother took Matthew and myself to the doctor's to find out why he wouldn't talk and why I was so stroppy when I spoke! I have no recollection of this as I only found out later on in life. The doctor blamed me and said that it seemed that I was so bossy I would not let Matthew speak! Nothing could be further from the truth. So it seemed to me that everyone was blaming me whatever I did, even when I tried to help. Another hitting probably followed this doctor's appointment I guess.

At home I would say to my mother, 'Matthew wants a biscuit', as he would whisper this to me if he was hungry. She would then reply with something sarcastic such as, 'I want – never gets.' What the hell that was all about I did not know? After all, if you want something, you want something. So we both ended up not even asking anymore as we weren't sure what she meant and no biscuit was offered to either Matthew or myself. We were hungry and I had already eaten some of those Vitamin C orange tablets from the bathroom cabinet as they looked like Smarties, but just tasted like an orange-flavoured sweet. They didn't really fill me up. I had to find something to eat. In my head I hatched a plan where I could get Matthew some food from the cupboards in the kitchen and hide it for us both.

It was a Sunday and my father was with Matthew in the garage at the bottom of the garden. My father used to try and keep out of the house at weekends as my mother made such dramas out of whatever anyone did. It was never right and she would go berserk at any little thing.

Everyone was out of the way. This was good for my plan, which was to go into the kitchen cupboard and steal some cooking chocolate and share it with Matthew. I would, of course, have the biggest share though. My mother was upstairs and all was quiet. I knew my mother used to keep slabs of cooking chocolate and also those chocolate polka drops used in homemade buns, in the kitchen cabinets. They were really nice and chocolatey. Unfortunately, they were in the cabinet high up on the wall that you had to reach to open, and I was too small to reach the handles. I found a small step or something similar to step onto, and managed to scramble and climb up onto the kitchen worktop. I was ready to reach the cabinet door for the chocolate, but as I reached up I nearly lost my balance, as the work surface was made from Formica so was quite smooth and slippery. I grabbed onto the cabinet unit door for balance and the whole lot of four or five cupboards literally fell off the wall, hit the worktop with an almighty crashing noise, and then smashed onto the floor.

It was like being in a nightmare; and I do not know how I avoided being hit by the falling heavy cabinets. I remember the sight of the long wooden cabinet cupboards now resting at an angle on the kitchen floor with all the doors wide open. There was self-raising flour and sugar burst out of their packets scattered all over the floor, other baking stuff such as jars of mincemeat, Atora suet, and jams smashed. Glass jars full of semolina and tapioca lay broken on the floor, their contents spilled everywhere, oh and a surprise light brown coloured biscuit tin that had been hidden from us, probably full of biscuits. There were big gaping holes on the tiled wall where the kitchen cabinets had been. I looked at the mess on the floor and my mother soon ran down the stairs to see what the crashing noise and crying was about. I ran out of the kitchen into the garden. To be honest I did not know where to run as nowhere was safe. Hopefully she wouldn't know it was me that had pulled the cupboard of the wall. I still hadn't got the bloody cooking chocolate, polka drops or anything to eat!

As if by coincidence, my father and Matthew came walking up the garden path and I was now crying – they probably heard the noise anyway of the cabinets smashing from the bottom of the garden. I recall my mother saying to my father that the cupboards didn't seem to be held onto the wall very securely and needed more screws in them and they could have fallen on anyone and killed them. I think she thought I was just walking into the kitchen and they just fell off the wall! Let her think that as it would save me from a beating. She blamed my father for his DIY skills – or lack of them! I certainly wasn't going to correct her.

In those days smoking was commonplace and almost expected in most households. My father used to smoke a lot, it was a bad, unhealthy and expensive habit, and when he was home the house used to smell of stale cigarettes and strong tobacco and make me feel ill. Those were the days when you could buy '20 Cadets' from Grandways super-market in Hessle Square, and in each packet of cigarettes you also got a voucher. Each voucher was worth a number of 'points', and the more points you collected the more expensive items you could order from a special 'Cadets' catalogue. My mother encouraged my father to smoke as she had seen items in the catalogue that would save her money from buying them herself from the shops. He would smoke over twenty cigarettes a day. So the ironic thing was that my father would spend HIS money on cigarettes (slowly killing himself in the process by smoking) but Mother would count the points on the vouchers and see what SHE could order from the catalogue for free.

There was method in her madness as she wanted Matthew and me out of the way and to keep us in the garden and not in the house with her. She ordered some outdoor toys so she could have peace and quiet in the house and just let us play in the garden, tenfoot or down the main road. We were able to have an orange Space Hopper each, which we loved, but Matthew went into the tenfoot with his and bounced on something sharp, so had to have his repaired with a bicycle puncture repair kit courtesy of my father. I also remember that I could have a pogo stick but there was only one in the catalogue and it wasn't that good. It only had a small spring so the pressure of going up on it continuously hurt the inside of both my feet. It didn't have much bounce. The other children I saw playing in the street had pogo sticks that had big springs on them and they could jump a lot higher on theirs than mine! But I didn't care as it got me out of the house and away from Mother.

We also somehow acquired swings and a see-saw. This was one long frame and had two plastic swings and a hanging see-saw. If that was coming from the Cadets catalogue then that would have been some serious smoking over the years to be able to collect enough points to purchase it. I suspect it may have come from a normal catalogue where you pay in monthly instalments such as Kays Catalogue, as my Aunty Linda had loads of catalogues Mother could buy from, and did Tupperware and later on Pippa Dee parties.

These were the days of frantically collecting vouchers and savings stamps on anything such as food and even petrol. I remember my grandma religiously collecting Green Shield stamps. When she bought anything at the local supermarket called Frank Dee's, a massive reel of stamps would be produced with her receipt and change at the till. She then had empty Green Shield books to stick the stamps onto page by page, allowing forty stamps per page. It kept me busy for ages, as you had to lick the glue on the back of the stamps and stick them in the book. When a full book was completed you could 'purchase' something from a catalogue, the more books you completed the more expensive items you could get e.g. lampshades, toys, electrical items etc. My grandma had loads of the completed books as she was always shopping, but I never knew what she actually got for free. As kids we just enjoyed licking and sticking the stamps onto each page.

I remember my father's very old moped. Nearly every Sunday morning he would travel from Hessle to Goddard Avenue in Hull to see his mother, father, and also his brother Colin who still lived in the same house. He had a tatty old crash helmet that he used, and also a smaller one that I was allowed to use. If Mother wanted rid of me for half a day she would ask my father to take me to my nana's house (we called my father's Mother Nana). I would sit on the moped behind my father, with my small crash helmet on (that probably wouldn't be any use if we actually did crash).

My arms weren't long enough to wrap them around my father's waist to hold on, so I had to put them in his pockets of his long coat and hope for the best. I actually quite enjoyed travelling on his moped. Although I had to confess that when he put his arm out to use as an indicator to go left or right, if I was bored I would also put my arm out, but in the opposite direction to confuse car drivers! I liked to live dangerously and am surprised we never got knocked off the moped by a car. I really should have been clinging on for dear life to be honest, but my father was a safe rider, and in those days there wasn't much traffic on the roads. I sometimes felt comfortable near my father and close to him. My mother had never hugged or kissed me that I could remember and if so, certainly not since Matthew arrived. The body heat from clinging onto my father on his moped was something I wasn't used to and it felt cosy, comforting and snug. I wished it could go on and on forever.

I didn't mind going to my nana's house as my nana and grandad left me alone, said 'hello', and had never hit me, but I still didn't feel comfortable there and I always felt 'in the way'. My father wasn't very close to his mother or father, so there was always a bit of tension there. He admitted to me that when he was young that their entertainment was to let him and his brother have boxing or wrestling matches in the front room on a Saturday night, until one of them was injured. That was their entertainment then before televisions were invented?! I was upset about this and couldn't understand why anyone would do this to their children, but then maybe it was the norm, after all Matthew and I were always subjected to violence in the home. My mind worked overtime – did people actually just have children to abuse them or watch them in pain? Who knew? I had no one to ask, so kept this thought to myself.

I was allowed in Nana's front room as they had a budgie that used to be quite vocal in his cage, and I was always fascinated by the blue feathers it had. When I finished talking to the budgie Nana would get me a drink of orange juice and my father a cup of tea, and I would then sit back in the cold front room and read the Sunday papers. It certainly increased my knowledge of the outside world. They always got the News of the World newspaper delivered. My mother and father never did; they got the Sunday People – which was a bit more reserved, shall we say. I do not think that my father realised that the News of the World was full of topless women and smutty comments. I think he would have been shocked. Still, it kept me quiet for an hour or two whilst they were all talking.

My nana and grandad in Hull were totally different from my other grandma in Hessle. They visited the local Social Club on Newland Avenue numerous times a week, having meals there, drinking, playing bingo and also having holidays abroad, especially to Spain, although the holidays abroad stopped when they were all involved in a serious car crash on the way to the airport. They were travelling in two taxis with my father's other brother, wife and their two adopted young children, Peter and Anne. Unfortunately, Anne, who was only very young, died in the car crash, and things were never really the same again for my nana and grandad who had doted on these two grandchildren. Not that I minded not being doted on, I never was anyone's favourite so was used to it. I was more annoyed with them that this was kept 'hush hush' as I had played games with Peter and Anne only recently when they were at my nana's house, and Anne's unfortunate, sudden death seemed to be a taboo subject. I wished the grown-ups would just talk straight and with honesty to me.

My grandad smoked like a chimney and his fingers were a yellowy brown colour from rolling his own cigarettes, and he also used to smoke a pipe occasionally. Their wallpaper and ceiling in both downstairs rooms was yellow with brown stains from the smoke in the air, and I must admit it was like walking into a chimney, full of smoke and stale smells. I hated it, but knew not to say anything. My clothes and hair would smell of the smoke as it lingered for hours afterwards. Their house was quite old fashioned compared to ours, it was a two-up, two-down terrace style property, with a large veranda with a downstairs toilet and an enclosed area where my Uncle Colin kept his motorbike. If you went to the toilet it always smelled of petrol and oil. My Uncle Colin lived there too and was always repairing his motorbike. To be honest the whole house's odour was a heady mix of petrol, oil and tobacco: you could probably get 'high' on it. I was surprised that by lighting a match for a cigarette or pipe that the whole place hadn't blown up. I was still fearful of fire in houses.

My father admitted to me that when he was younger he wanted to leave home as soon as possible and get away from his parents excessive drinking and having to do things he didn't want to do (I presumed fighting his brother). I noticed that my father only had an alcoholic drink at Christmas time and even then he wasn't really bothered. He enjoyed a Mackeson can of stout and my mother enjoyed a small sherry. They let me have a small mouthful of sherry once at Christmas and it nearly burned my throat! It was horrendous. How anyone could enjoy this type of drink was beyond me. My nana and grandad must have an acquired taste for it, I thought.

My other grandma in Hessle (my mother's mother) was the total opposite in her ways. She did not drink or smoke, certainly did not read any newspapers such as the News of the World, or celebrate Christmas or birthdays. This was the start of her being converted to a Jehovah's Witness that would cause so much friction between the family.

As I got older I became more inquisitive and kept asking questions about anything from the human body to learning about animals. I also loved going into the garage with my father when he was trying to mend his moped or just pottering about with electrical stuff, trying to repair it. I hated having to ask anything as I was trying not to talk so I would not get told off, but sometimes questions would just sort of 'burst' out of my mouth and I could not stop them. It was the questions that children ask and usually started with the one of the words who/what/when/where/why/how? My father tried to give me answers to the questions but admittedly he didn't know the correct answers. Remember, this was the time before the internet. I had a dictionary and some Janet and John books in my bedroom but they weren't going to tell me about how big is an elephant or how an eye sees.

My mother had less patience with me. She gave me a nickname of 'Moaning Minnie', so every time I asked a question she would say 'oh Moaning Minnie is at it again.'

This was her way of deflecting the question I was asking, as she didn't know the answer. Bearing in mind I was reluctant to speak anyway at home, this just reinforced my views that I would never speak or ask any questions again. I decided not to respond to any questions or demands my mother would also ask or say, so I was continually slapped by her on the back of my legs for being 'rude'. I seriously could not win, and it frustrated me. She complained when I spoke and also complained when I didn't. What the hell was I supposed to do?

My father was not happy with her for causing my dilemma, and now also creating a nickname. He, very unusually for once, took my side and said to my mother that if I had a nickname then she had to have one too. Her nickname was 'Skippy' (as in the bush kangaroo), as all she had done since the beginning of the year when my father temporarily lost his job, was tut at everything he or anyone had, or hadn't done. The tutting was exasperating and instead of my mother asking why we had done something she would just raise her eyes to the ceiling and tut, then lower her eyes and look down on us like a piece of dirt on her shoe. Her tutting, to show her disapproval, was funny for the first time but subsequent times it got a very repetitive and boring. The laughable thing was that she didn't know she was even doing it; it came as second nature to her now.

Matthew and I actually loved the original Skippy, which was a children's television programme set near Sydney, Australia, that told stories and adventures of a little boy and his pet kangaroo named Skippy. The noises that Skippy the kangaroo made were just like short tutting noises when he was trying to talk. Skippy also did other noises like growls and clucking, but we chose to remember the tutting ones. Every time Mother tutted we would sing or hum the 'Skippy song'. You know the one, 'Skippy, Skippy, Skippy the bush kangaroo ...' she hated it but she started my nickname: if you can't handle it – then don't dish it out ... My father was the one who eventually told us to stop singing the Skippy song as it now annoyed Mother. But I observed it was still okay for her to call me Moaning Minnie! Mother even told other people such as my aunty that I was a Moaning Minnie. I did notice that at school I was never called a Moaning Minnie, as I seemed to ask relevant questions and the teacher always tried to answer them. It seemed that my nickname at home was because my mother could not be bothered to talk to me anymore, and did not know anything intellectual anyway, and didn't even want to hear me.

I didn't care. I was used to my own company by now and liked it that way. I learned to keep out of Mother's way by walking out of a room if she walked in, or by playing in the garden on the swings, even in the freezing cold. Unfortunately another 'spanner in the works' was my cousin Carol, the one that my mother wished I was a clone of, and basically wished she had given birth to instead of me. Apparently my grandma had taken Carol to ballet and tap lessons at the town hall in Hessle, and Carol had loved it. Well she would do, I secretly thought, she liked being centre of attention and showing off. I certainly didn't feel the need to show off, but clearly my family loved a show-off.

The next time my grandma took Carol to ballet and tap-dancing lessons, I also had to tag along, join in, and act like I wanted to be there. I hated ballet. I wasn't the correct shape, size or didn't have a great deal of balance. My mother had bought me a pair of black ballet pumps to compete with Carol's, but they were too tight for me and as my feet had high arches, were painful to wear. My toes were clawed under. But I had to be grateful I had been given them. My mother always had this persona that to the outside world it looked like we had everything and we were well looked after, but that wasn't the case. We rarely got anything new and if we did it was from the cigarette vouchers catalogue.

I didn't mind tap dancing, it seemed like fun, was good exercise and it was noisy and you could bash your feet down as hard as you liked on the stage (well I did anyway). I loved my tap shoes. The stroppy woman who taught the class told me off for being so heavy footed 'like an elephant', she quoted. Well I wanted to be heavy footed as it seemed to get some of the anger out of me to be honest. I didn't really care for the arm stretching and posing that was also involved in tap dancing. I was more of an early 'Riverdance' performer, you know, arms by my side but feet fast and furious with my tap shoes on. I certainly had the stamina to do that as I loved sport and gymnastics at school so it came easily. I thought I was good but unfortunately no one else in the class did, they were so gentile and calming. I must have seemed like an elephant on a sugar rush when I danced, and I was the only one that was red in the face from putting extra effort into it. Still, I had been told to go to the lessons so I would continue them, plus the added bonus was that I wasn't at home being hit.

I trained for over six months and it was okay I suppose. Every Saturday morning my grandma would take Carol and myself to the town hall for lessons and we were building up to the Christmas dance performance where family and friends were invited. My grandma would stay and watch us both rehearse and she was kind to Carol as Carol wanted to show her that she was the best. I just seemed to be ignored, although my grandma was sometimes generous and bought us both a small bottle of pop and chocolate bar each, which is more than I would have got from my mother. The other children around me seemed to be more outspoken and dramatic than myself and used to wear make-up, even though they were only about six to seven years old. The bright red lipstick and blusher they wore seemed to be like my mother's lipstick and wasn't very attractive. I was quite good at memorising the ballet and tap routines we had to do, boring as they were, whereas the others could hardly remember their own names never mind a dance routine set to boring, monotonous, monotone piano music. They were right little divas in the class and I couldn't cope with those people; I had enough dramas at home and I certainly didn't want to see it elsewhere.

It came to the middle of November and the stroppy dance class teacher was getting excited, and saying to bring in your money next week for costumes to wear for the Christmas Show. She would provide the material and patterns and your mother had to make your costume. That was debatable about the sewing and Mother, but I had to go along with it. Unfortunately, the next weekend I was ill. I suffered from a really bad throat, could hardly speak and had a bad tickly cough, so didn't go to dance class. To be honest I felt so ill I couldn't have made it, and maybe I even had tonsillitis, but in those days you rarely went to the doctors, except in an emergency. So I just suffered and stayed at home, coughing and spluttering to myself in my bedroom.

The following Saturday I had nearly recovered and was there at the dance class, money in my hand ready for the material for my costume. Stroppy woman was sat at her piano on her stool, and said to me 'You missed your turn last week to pay, so you cannot have a costume.' I was gutted and remember going to the old-fashioned toilets there and crying. That starting my cough off again even more! I just sat in the toilets, crying and coughing and never even came out of there until the class finished. After all, why should I practice anymore when I wasn't going to be in the Christmas Show? I was absolutely fuming, especially when Carol could have got my stuff last weekend if we had known it was the only weekend to pay, but it wasn't her fault. After that I gave up with dance class or anything to do with dancing, my mother or grandma didn't seem that bothered, they were too busy gushing over Carol and watching her practice to notice me. The worse thing was that I had to go with my grandma a few weeks later and watch the bloody Christmas Show with Carol performing in it on stage. Talk about rubbing your nose in it! To top it all, my mother was given a photo of Carol in a red tutu doing a flipping curtsey, which she has kept to this day, whereas photos of myself are very few. The lesson I learned from this was do not trust anyone, child or adult, and certainly do not do any hobby or activity that relies on and involves other people! That was me done; I wasn't going to be a team player anymore. Stuff the bloody dance class and silly girly routines.

It was the next school summer holidays and Matthew and I were bored. I think he was just about to begin school so hopefully he would get some education and be able to communicate more. We were both in the back garden just messing about, playing with his toy cars in the mud, doing nothing dangerous or bad. My mother was also there but in a foul mood with herself for no reason. I remember she was near the garage at the bottom of the garden with a paintbrush in her hand. I cannot even remember what she was painting, she loved to paint anything she could for some reason. Suddenly she walks up the garden path and starts shouting that she has had enough of us and is going. She throws the paintbrush somewhere in the garden and the next thing she is walking through the house, out of the front door and up the street.

I start to feel the panic rising, mainly that my father will go absolutely ballistic when he comes home and finds out that Mother has gone because of Matthew and I. I ask Matthew to chase after her, as he is her favourite and she wouldn't want to upset him. I open the front door and the porch door and let him run after her with his shoes half on and shoe laces undone. I follow closely behind as I know she won't want to see me. Matthew tells Mother in his stuttering, crying voice that she has to come home as he can't tie his shoe laces. Mother looks at him, he is crying and upset as he isn't sure why she's leaving. I think she realises that the neighbours can see her and it doesn't look good that her two children are running after her in the street, so she turns round and walks back home.

To this day I still do not know what we had done wrong. I presume nothing. Maybe she just wanted to have her own life without us as she kept saying we were both mistakes. I was seriously confused. Did this happen to all families? What if she had left us and my father had come back from work and it was after 7pm? Matthew was young and she would have abandoned him, and myself. I didn't know what we could eat and what we were supposed to do. I wasn't even sure how to put the television on, or should we just stay outside on the swings? I had so many questions but no one to ask, I daren't even ask Doreen next door, not that she would have minded but she was busy with work and looking after her mother. I do not even know if Mother told my father that she had walked out on us – probably not. Matthew and I were now both scared of being alone.

My father always had a small radio in the bathroom that he used to switch on in the mornings when he was getting shaved and ready for work. The bathroom was next to my bedroom so the radio used to always wake me up at about

6am–6.30am as my father was a bit deaf, but never admitted it. Every morning he would listen to Radio Humberside which, for a child, was the most boring of radio stations as it had more talking with phone-ins and conversations and boring people's opinions than music. However, in this year one song struck home to make me think that this was the reality and this was definitely the norm.

The song on the radio was called 'Chirpy Chirpy, Cheep Cheep' by a group named 'Middle of the Road'. The lyrics consisted of the words: 'where's your mama gone ... far far away. Woke up this morning and my mama was gone ...'

To me, a young child going through these periods of uncertainty and bordering on neglect, it confirmed to me that this was normal, waking up one morning and your mother had gone! After all a pop group had actually written about it also so it must be true for everyone, or so I thought! I knew then that Matthew and I had to get on with life and if Mother left then it was okay, as everyone's mother did it. So there would be no more running after her in the street, begging her to stay. We had to let her go as that's what the song said that mothers do. For a young child that was now clear in my mind. I would now mentally and emotionally distance myself from her.

CHAPTER 7

Excitement and Punishment

In this year, 1972, my father had improved his mode of transport from the old moped to a green Morris Minor car. On a Sunday he decided to take Matthew and me out in the car, to see Nana in Hull to give my mother a 'break', as he called it.

When we got to Nana's she mentioned that there was a children's miniature railway set up in the park down the road at the junction of Goddard Avenue and Chanterlands Avenue. My father didn't need telling twice. We were bundled back into the car and he drove off to find this park and the train, telling her we would be back later on.

When we got there, there were already children and parents standing on the grass, watching a small train go round a temporary railway track in the park. The train wasn't big, just the size where a child could sit on it, legs astride it. It probably carried about twelve children at once. Grown-ups weren't allowed as it wouldn't probably take the weight of them, except the train driver of course, he was driving at the front and had his back to us all. The track seemed to go on forever and went in a large circle at the outskirts of the park and under trees.

My father paid the train driver for Matthew and me to go on the train, we hopped on, and it set off slowly. It was quite exciting and as it got faster I could feel the rush of the wind against my face and the driver was blowing the train whistle, it was really quite good and exciting for an eight-year-old.

There were a few other children on the ride also and we were all laughing and giggling when we set off and got more speed up on the track. We were certainly getting value for money as we were going round and round the park numerous times with the train whistle blowing as it approached the adults, and we all waved each time we passed them.

By now, I was getting a bit bored, so decided that the next time the train went underneath a big overhanging tree, we would each try and pull a leaf off it. So I shouted back to the other children that next time we went under a tree we would reach up and grab a leaf then compare who had the biggest leaf. Unfortunately, this activity did not go to plan. As we all reached up and leant over to one side, the train derailed and came off the tracks, presumably as the weight of everyone was at one side and not balanced anymore. I hadn't really thought of that.

There were children now lying on the grass crying, some still clutching their leaves, others had twigs in their hands. The train was on its side also; luckily no one had been squashed or hurt by it. The driver of the train was okay and didn't realise what was happening as he was obviously facing forwards and had his own carriage. I heard him say that he had never had this happen before. Luckily no one was seriously injured and we all picked ourselves up off the ground, with the train still on its side, the driver still stunned and now trying to put his train back onto the track. Children were running to their parents, who were at the other side of the park. I kept quiet as I secretly knew it was me that had caused this 'freak accident' and was scared in case one of the children said it was my idea, then I would be told off by my father and then Mother. Although it sounds funny, it could have had serious repercussions. I only wanted fun and laughter, it was not malicious. I made a mental note to not do something so stupid again. We went back to Nana's to recover and tell her, with excitement, what had happened!

These were the old-fashioned days in the early 1970s. My mother was still using a twin tub for washing clothes. She refused to buy an automatic washing machine and also a modern tumble dryer. She really was a martyr and enjoyed all the drama of huffing and puffing when washing clothes in a twin tub. We knew never to go into the kitchen if she was washing as we would get the brunt of it. If it was too wet and rainy to hang out the clothes after being washed, then she would use a wooden fold up clothes horse and put it in front of the open coal fire. The problem was that some clothes got scorch marks from the heat of the fire, or burns holes from the coal spitting out from the fire onto the clothes and burning them, especially those made of polyester material.

The money situation from last year seemed to have been forgotten about and my mother had bought (or acquired) a Flatley clothes dryer. This was basically a free-standing metal box on wheels standing about three and a half feet high with a metal lid that lifted up. Inside were wooden rods, a bit like spindles, about six or eight of them, each two feet long that slotted into notches in the top of the dryer. A bit like a 'hanging file' drawer in an office, but this was on a larger scale. Over the wooden rods you would drape your damp clothes or sheets etc, then plug it in. There was an electric element at the bottom that would heat up and warm the washing. There was no timer on it or heat settings, it was just remembering that you had switched it on, so you could switch it off again before it set the clothes, or itself, on fire! I am sure it would have been simpler to have just bought a tumble dryer like other households had, but my mother was stubborn and liked the drama of it all.

This Flatley dryer would be our worst nightmare. We were

always being punished for speaking and/or being naughty, then being hit by Mother's hands, along with anything else that was in reaching distance thrown at us that may hurt e.g. slippers, books or anything handy, we had got used to that; we now had an additional contender.

Unfortunately, the flipping Flatley dryer was dual purpose in our house – clothes dryer and a punishment or torture tool. I still remember the red weal marks on my legs from being hit with those solid wooden rods. If ever we were naughty, Mother would go into the kitchen and Matthew and I would look at each other, knowing what may be happening next. We would hear the metal lid of the dryer opening and we would try and run up the stairs, but we had nowhere to hide. The stick would come down on us wherever she wanted, our back, legs, backside. The pain was horrendous. It was like torture. If she was feeling really stressed and had the red-mist rage she would keep hitting us over and over again as she could not stop herself. We felt that if she hit us to death then at least we'd have no more pain. If my father was home, which was rare, he would try and stop her hitting us by telling her she had gone too far. But he was a weak man most of the time, and he wanted a quiet life, so let her rule the house. This would go on for years to come and I resented even being in the same room or even the same house as Mother, so tried to always avoid it.

Now looking back at school photos, I had what I call the 'far away, exasperated look', probably because I was wishing I was bloody far away, preferably another country or a different world. Matthew was never hit as hard as myself, after all he wasn't even five years old, but I seemed to take the punishment of it whether it was me or him that had done something wrong, or not even done anything at all. I remember getting the blame for just sitting there on the settee and doing nothing. Well, I wasn't allowed to speak in the house and when I did speak I was called Moaning Minnie, then told that children 'should be seen and not heard'. I was always in a no-win situation. Obviously my parents didn't even want to see me as it annoyed them. So the saying should be that children 'should not be seen OR heard', I thought to myself. I was told that I got the blame as I was the eldest child and 'should know better', even when it wasn't my fault! I was bordering on having serious anxiety and stress issues, and spent most of the time crying in secret. I needed someone to help and understand me, but there was no one there. I even resented little things such as my photo being taken by the school or by my father, as it was supposed to represent a 'happy time or a happy family', which we certainly weren't. My school photos were horrendous and I had that glazed, worried expression, but no one seemed to ask if I was okay.

Spring and summer times were okay as we could play on the swings and see-saw outside, but we were told by Mother that the other neighbours' children could not play on them in case they broke them, and that 'they had their own gardens to play in'. Matthew and I were quite isolated at this point as we could see and hear other children playing in their own gardens, but couldn't join in and they couldn't join us either. I did feel safer outside the house, though, as I knew that Mother wouldn't hit us outside with the sticks, as I am sure the neighbours, especially Doreen, would go mad with her, and Mother had a façade to keep up with us pretending to be the perfect family. I didn't even care if it was cold or raining, outside was the safest place for us to be.

CHAPTER 8

Resent and Repent

A long with the so-called 'perfect family' was the perfect holiday. Over the next few years we would holiday only at Hornsea in my grandma's caravan. The site I had visited some three years previously.

Hornsea was, and still is, a remote seaside resort on the east coast in the East Riding of Yorkshire and only about twenty-two miles from Hessle. But by public bus it was a long, bumpy, slow trip across the county of East Riding or East Yorkshire, as it was named then. It took well over an hour and a half to get there, if not two hours – in a car it would only be about thirty–forty minutes travelling time maximum. I was not a good traveller and was easily travel sick. The bus route went from Hessle via Anlaby and Cottingham and into Beverley, then stopped for about half an hour in Beverley bus station, before travelling onto remote locations such as Tickton, Leven, Sigglesthorne and eventually arriving at Hornsea having gone past the massive mere.

No wonder I always used to be travel sick by the time we got to Hornsea by bus, after that horrendous nightmare journey. Luckily the caravan park was nearby when I got off at Hornsea bus terminal, at the top of Cliff Road, so I didn't have far to walk in my nauseous state. I used to try and contain myself by trying not to faint, then I would sometimes collapse outside the caravan and try and sit on the caravan steps. Sometimes I was actually sick on the bus and my mother made me take a small plastic bucket with me for such an occasion. I hated that bus with all the stopping, starting and the diesel fumes that seemed to enter the bus at the rear, making me even more nauseous. I'd rather stay at home by myself, but this didn't seem to be an option at my age of nine years old. I dreaded arriving at Hornsea then dreaded the journey back, so could never relax.

My mother used to give me travel sickness tablets at home but I could never swallow them anyway, and the stress of having to take a tablet such as Kwells made me even more anxious. I had to crunch them to swallow them and they tasted rancid. Even chewing the tablets made me physically sick in the house, and that was before we had even set off. I used to try and spit the tablet out but there was nowhere to really spit it out such as into a plant pot or anything. After attempting to take the tablets, that made me so thirsty, my mother, brother and I had to walk from Belvedere Road, with all our holdalls, to Hessle Square bus station and wait for the Hornsea bus that only ran either once or twice a day. I hated it and even walking to the bus station made me feel sick in the stomach.

The static caravan my grandma bought for family holidays was located at the top of Cliff Road, Hornsea, almost opposite the bus terminal and Northern Dairies milk depot. There was a holiday chalet park called Golden Imp right opposite the caravan site at the edge of a cornfield. I was always jealous of the people staying there as the chalets were wooden and had electricity and a bathroom. I knew this, as sometimes I wandered onto the public bridle path at the side of the cornfield, and could see inside the chalets that they had proper bedrooms with a full size bed, small portable televisions and a drain for water – unlike grandma's caravan that had none of these.

I knew that the caravan was my grandma's but didn't really understand why she had it, plus how she could afford it, as she never worked? My grandad must have left her a shedload of money in his will, as she also had a semi-detached house in a prime location near Hessle Square and didn't seem to have any money worries. She was a bit calmer and placid than my mother was, but did irrational things at times, and could be violent towards us.

There wasn't, and still isn't, a lot at Hornsea to entertain children. It had the famous Hornsea Potteries that you could visit and use the children's playground, and there was the factory where you could see the famous Hornsea Pottery crockery being made (if you paid an admission fee). There was also Hornsea Mere where you could hire rowing boats, or just walk across the grassy areas along with massive geese and swans that hissed and chased you. Then there was Hall Garth Park which had a large playground surrounded by acres of grass that was also a golf course. Heading up Cliff Road towards the caravan site was Hornsea Floral Hall, a sort of evening venue for family nights, discos and other entertainment, complete with a bowling green on the side of it and a large pub nearby overlooking the beach.

There were also a few amusement arcades on the seafront, I grew to love one called Past-times, it had penny machines there and we were allowed a few pennies to keep us quiet. Sometimes my mother or grandma (if she came with us) even bought us a bag of chips from the chippy to share on the way back to the caravan. We had to walk on the clifftop as it was the quickest way back, even though it was dark, the cliffs were eroding away and dangerous.

The caravan was situated on a site that kept changing its name, so I can never remember what the site was called. The static caravan my grandma had was located at the edge of the site and was parallel to a street that had prefabs with older people living in them, there was a small dividing wire fence and also a ditch at our side of the caravan site. The ditch was about five or six feet deep and full of nettles, weeds and grass clippings that the people in the prefabs used to throw over the fence, and I'm sure it had rats and mice living in it also.

It was like something out of an early 1960s comedy show, the caravan was painted cream with a horizontal orange stripe, it wasn't even a good paint job and I think it was just emulsioned on. It had two metal stable doors, with one door into the tiny kitchen and the other one into the room area (I will use the word 'room' loosely!).

There was no electricity. There were three gas mantle lights to light the whole of the caravan. These were 'bulbs' made of out a material similar to gauze and attached to a gas fitting. You had to turn on the lights individually by turning a knob and letting the gas come through slowly, then lighting the gauze mantle with a long match or wick. If you were too rough with the lit match, then the mantle would pierce and break and there would be a whoosh of flames as, in effect, you were lighting a live gas pipe. I hated it there at night time, especially when my grandma tried to light the mantle lights as she could never do it first time and it smelled of escaping gas. I tried to sit near the door, for an easy escape; after all, my mother had set fire to my bedroom at Salisbury Street and I was petrified of fire and matches but, of course, I didn't confess this to my mother or anyone. I learned never to confess to a weakness or something you were scared of.

As there was no electricity, we had no television, fridge or freezer or any mod-cons. Basically anything with an electrical plug was unusable. We had a small gas oven/grill and also a two-ring gas hob to cook on.

There was also one stand-alone gas fire that was not even

attached to the floor, so could easily be knocked or tipped over by accident. The gas lights and gas fire were connected to an outside Calor gas cylinder and there was always a gas smell in the caravan, which frightened me all the time in case it exploded. It was known on the caravan site that some caravans had actually blown up due to gas leaks; this unnerved me even more! Especially when I found out that this was actually true, and one caravan very near us had exploded, and they had lost their large Lassie-type dogs that were in the caravan at the time. Luckily they were both eventually found on the beach nearby, shaking and scared out of their bloody wits! I knew how they felt!

There was no running water in grandma's caravan, so no toilet, bathroom, wash basin or any such luxuries. There were standpipes around the caravan site to allow you to fill up large water canisters with freezing cold water. Even the taps weren't the conventional ones, and were the push type ones that allowed you to get about half a litre of water out only in one go. You usually only used standpipes during a drought to restrict your water use, not on a paid caravan site! You could not put too much water in the canisters anyway as you couldn't carry it back to the caravan as they became too heavy. So that was our water supply. We would put the half-full cold water container at the side of the sink in the kitchen. The sink wasn't plumbed in, so the dirty water just came out below via a piece of small hosepipe, out into a strategically based builder's bucket that needed emptying a few times a day.

There were two toilet blocks on the site, both split into male and female. Each of these had six toilets in them and two hand basins, but no hand soap, paper towels and certainly no showers, just cold water, again with the push taps, to avoid using too much water. There weren't any plugs for the sinks, so you couldn't even fill the hand basin with water to get washed. There weren't any electrical plug sockets there either, so no chance of using a hairdryer. We had to take our own toilet paper to the toilet block, so everyone knew when you were going for a wee! The only toilet paper available in the toilet block was what we used to call 'Shiny Jack' – I do not know why we called it that, but I can imagine why. It was the Izal medicated toilet roll that scratched your bum as one side was like glossy photo paper and the other was like thick tracing paper that didn't really clean wipe, it just spread! The caravan site owners were so bloody stingy with resources that even the loo roll holders on the wall were the metal ones that you only could remove one or two pieces of Izal loo roll at a time and then it 'locked'. You had to reverse the toilet roll to get more off it. The caravan site managers must have thought that people actually wanted to use their facilities even if they hadn't a caravan on the site, and eventually put a lock on the toilet block and issued keys to each caravan owner. If anyone such as a member of the public actually wanted to use those facilities, heaven help them! I'd rather pee myself or do it in the sea. I remember my grandma getting numerous keys cut for the toilet block as we kept leaving them in the toilet block, then couldn't get back in again. We had to have them attached to our wrists with a piece of elastic so we didn't lose them!

There were lights outside the toilet block, but were on a timer set by the camp owners and automatically switched off by about 10pm, so if you needed to use the loos after this time, you had to take the toilet block key, loo roll and also a torch. Anything could have happened to any child in those days, but no one seemed to think anything of it.

When my grandma looked after us at the caravan, she luckily realised the toilet situation and the possible danger that we could be in, so bought a child's pink potty that we could all use, in the kitchen area of the caravan, to have a wee in the night! In the morning she would empty the contents of the potty into the nettle ditch next to the caravan! I was flaming nine years old and having to use a potty at night. For God's sake!

In the middle section of the caravan there was a pull-down double bed for the adults. There was a curtain separating this area and the front of the caravan that had a small seating area for about four people, this seating area was to double up at night time into a bedroom. It was not very private and the seating area smelled of the sweaty sandy bodies that had sat there during the day. All we had was a pillow each and a heavy blanket that smelled really fusty as they were all stored under the seating area in the caravan, and were probably never washed from year to year. The heavy blanket was okay to start off with, but by midnight the caravan was freezing and the heavy blanket was not enough to keep anyone warm. I never had a good night's sleep there. I may as well have been sleeping outside as my feet were always cold. Caravan insulation in those days was non-existent, and there was no such thing as double glazing in caravans or central heating. To be honest the night time in that caravan was like being inside a fridge!

If my two cousins stayed, then they sometimes slept on the floor. That was even colder as the carpet had no underlay, and also there was sand and dust on the thin carpet. As we couldn't use an electric vacuum cleaner, we relied on a push-along carpet sweeper that didn't exactly sweep or clean any floor. It is a surprise that none of us had any breathing or lung conditions from all the dust, dirt and sand that we were actually laying on in the night for hours on end. Either way, wherever you slept, on the floor or on the seating area, it was bloody freezing.

There were two orange skylights on the roof, to allow some ventilation in during the day, but as they were only made out of thin Perspex, this added to the draughts and being freezing cold at night even if they were closed. It also let the bright sunlight in during summer time first thing in the morning, so anyone there was lucky to get about four hours sleep. Then the seagulls would be landing on the caravan roof, walking up and down and squawking in the early hours of the morning. This caravan was supposed to be used for a relaxing holiday but seemed like torture and anything but relaxing.

My father always had an excuse that he could not come to the caravan. He was always working, or so he said. He was probably just enjoying the time at home by himself, and I couldn't blame him, but we were left with Mother in a small space with definitely nowhere to run if she turned on us. My grandma would sometimes take Matthew and I to the caravan, on the bus, along with my cousins. I didn't mind that too much as she wouldn't hit us as much as Mother. My younger cousin seemed to get the wrath of it instead, but I couldn't do anything to help, and knew how he felt.

My grandma trusted Carol and myself to go across Cliff Road to Northern Dairies and buy glass bottles of sterilised milk for breakfast cereal. As we had no fridge, we had to buy sterilised milk, known as steri milk, as it lasted longer and didn't need to be cooled in a fridge. It is an acquired taste and there is nothing worse than milk at room temperature. To this day I will remember the taste: it was creamy but also a bit rancid. I have never bought it since!

After breakfast, Carol and I were allowed to walk into Hornsea on our own. We would even walk as far as Hornsea Potteries and used to look through the windows of the factory and then watch the ducks on the small duck pond. Other days we would walk to Hornsea Mere and we found a small bakery nearby and used to ask if they had any stale bread for free to feed the geese and ducks on the mere. The geese must have seemed quite big to the height of us both but we weren't frightened of them. We always looked through the old café windows at the mere and wished we had pocket money to afford such luxuries as a bottle of pop or chocolate bar to share. But we never did; we did without. We would spend hours just watching the rowing boats and yachts on the mere and feeding the birds with stale bread.

By the time we got back to the caravan it was nearly teatime and I was usually sunburned and as red as a lobster, as I had fair skin. My grandma used to tell me to put on some suncream, but all she had was Nivea sun factor 2 – no protection for a child that needed sun factor 50. These were the days before awareness of damage to skin from the sun's UVB rays and skin cancer. In fact, my grandma used to put margarine on any sunburn we had. I could never understand that, as in effect it would heat up and make me feel even worse. I used to think she was a bit mad for doing that and I would wash it off with freezing cold, but soothing, water from the standing pipes on the caravan site.

For tea my grandma would make us all Cremola for dessert as 'it is Carol's favourite'. This was like an Angel Delight creamy dessert made with milk and to be honest it was okay, but for goodness sake, she had other grandchildren but it was always 'Carol this ... Carol that ... Carol's favourite.' Carol could never do a thing wrong as she was very sneaky and blamed other people. I soon realised her games. She always acted the victim or would cry deliberately to get attention, which she always seemed to get.

One day at the caravan Carol was really bragging and showing off outside the caravan to my grandma. She was dancing around pretending to be a ballerina and just acting like a spoilt brat in general. My grandma was watching her from inside the caravan from the side window and clapping and encouraging her. I was sickened by the showing off and prancing about outside. I hated show-offs. As soon as my grandma looked away, I gave Carol a massive shove and pushed her into the ditch of nettles at the side of the caravan. I knew it was malicious and nasty but I just wanted it to stop. I wanted to be alone and away from all the showing off. Of course Carol screamed, cried and clambered out of the ditch – stung by the nettles and possibly smelling of wee as my grandma threw the wee from pink potty in the ditch every morning. Carol was ushered into the caravan by my grandma, the door slammed shut, and I was locked out of it. I knocked on the metal caravan door but no one answered and then the curtains were closed so no one could see me. Not that I cared, I would find somewhere else to go to. In my mind as an eight-year-old I thought there may be an empty caravan I could stay in by myself, but I knew there would be nothing on our caravan site as it was only a small site, so I had to go elsewhere.

I walked from our caravan site and turned right, and walked further up the incline on Cliff Road away from Hornsea. I passed the red telephone box on the right and walked up a bit more to the next caravan site, then walked past that and went to the next caravan site even further up the hill. This looked a bigger and better caravan site than ours. I walked into the site. It had small shops including a newsagents, launderette and an indoor area where young children and teenagers were playing table tennis and just sat talking. Within this was a café area. I could see this from the outside as there were large glass windows. This was my kind of caravan site that I wanted to stay in; you could walk from your caravan and just mooch around playing table tennis and talking. There were no such facilities at our site and it was boring, I did not want to sit on the beach all day or stay at the mere as I got sunburned quickly and it hurt. I would much rather play table tennis.

The caravan site owners on my grandma's site did allow goods vans to visit daily. One van was full of newspapers and magazines and the driver used to sound his horn to let the caravan owners know that he was parking up on the site for a few minutes. Then each Friday night there was the chip shop van that also used to come onto the caravan site to sell fish and chips. Along with the ice cream van of course. We were never allowed any of these things although, if my father was staying at the caravan (which was rare), he would sometimes buy the local newspaper and even a morning paper, even though Mother would tut at him for spending money! Yes, this other caravan site was so much better.

I had a look around the site by myself and no one stopped me, so I entered the table tennis room and sat there for what seemed like ages just watching people. Eventually I thought I had better walk back to our caravan site. I knew I would have to apologise to Carol (through gritted teeth) before I was let into the caravan again. I mooched around the site once more, looking to see if there were any empty caravans that were unlocked, but I daren't try the door handles as I knew I would get into trouble. So I took a slow walk back down the dusty, sandy road with fields of corn on the right. I was thirsty and hadn't eaten for what seemed like ages but I was used to that even at home, why should being at Hornsea be any different? I braved knocking on the door of grandma's caravan and had to face the wrath of it all, being shown Carol's arms all covered in nettle stings. She was still sniffling and rubbing her eyes to make them even redder, for sympathy. Such a big drama, but I knew I had done wrong, although it was funny to see at the time. If she had been hit, like we had been at home, by mother with the Flatley dryer sticks, then she would have something to cry about! She was such a cry-baby and knew how to get her own way. I was otherwise ignored for the rest of the night and the holiday. Oh well, I was used to that also, ignored by my grandma as well as my mother, it was no great deal.

CHAPTER 9

Repulsive and Compulsive

It was 1973 and back home my father was still doing DIY projects in the house ever since we had moved in. I think he did it to get away from the house and Mother, as all he seemed to do on a Saturday, if he wasn't working, was joinery and other menial things in the large garage. On Sundays he would still sometimes go into Hull to his mother's house, but not quite as much. His classic clumsiness included leaving a soldering iron plugged in, in the shed, and Matthew trying to pick it up with his hand – ouch! This resulted in blisters all over the palm of his hand and Matthew screaming in pain all the way up the garden path!

My father had spent months making a frame for a homemade wardrobe for my bedroom. Even thought it was for my bedroom, it wasn't actually for me, it was for Mother to put her items in. The wardrobe had a big wooden frame and stretched from floor to ceiling with wooden sliding doors. The wardrobe also hid the old-fashioned copper hot water tank that was in my bedroom. That took up about a third of the wardrobe space anyway. The other side of the wardrobe was used by my mother for her storage, e.g. for the Christmas decorations and the spare bedsheets. So in effect I had one small area of the wardrobe to myself, not even a fifth, and that was it. Not that I had a lot to put in it anyway. Maybe a spare pair of plimsolls, or my junior school clothes.

Since this wardrobe had been built, my father had added extra shelves near the hot water tank cupboard as my mother had suddenly wanted to put her nightdress and dressing gown in there each day so they would allegedly 'warm up' during the day with the heat of the water cylinder. Why she just didn't get a hot water bottle instead and put that, and her nightdress, in her own bed I will never know. But she was cunning and now had an excuse to annoy me even when I was in bed trying to sleep.

Every night between 9pm and 9.30pm, depending on what television programmes were on and she was watching downstairs, Mother would think nothing of waking me up by opening my bedroom door, switching the bedroom light on, walking to the wardrobe and noisily opening the sliding door then fumbling about for her winceyette nightdress and my father's pyjamas. Then she would close the wardrobe door and walk out as if nothing had happened. She sometimes would leave my bedroom light on deliberately so I would have to get out of bed to turn it off. She was such a bitch. She even used to come into my bedroom naked, after going into the bathroom first. What the hell was all that about? I will never know.

Her white, wobbly, flabby, overweight, whale-like body was certainly not the same as the naked women's bodies I'd seen photographed in the News of the World newspaper at my nana's house! She was far more than twice their size and looked twice as ugly. I was always wide awake after this nightly occurrence as, if I complained that she woke me up, I would be the one that was moaning again. 'Bloody Moaning Minnie, she's at it again,' she would loudly complain to my father when she went into their bedroom to get dressed into her night clothes. 'SHE never stops bloody moaning!' she would shout. Nearly the whole street could hear her.

You would have thought that once you had gotten your children to sleep the last thing you would want to do was to wake them up again. She was seriously psychotic and deranged and said horrible things deliberately to provoke me, so she could turn on me. I was too clever for her mind games, and she knew it.

If Matthew and I had been allegedly 'naughty' during the day, I dreaded night time. My mother now had the perfect excuse and would come into my bedroom to get her nightdress from the tank cupboard and then turn on me, shouting anything abusive. She even once shouted to me that she hoped I would 'rot in hell'. She would say these things to make me cry, so I wouldn't be able to sleep. I admit that I had (and still have) a serious case of anxiety issues, bordering on post-traumatic stress disorder. Wouldn't anyone though, having to listen to that verbal abuse every night? That was only part one of the night-time ritual, then I would have to endure part two – the physical abuse.

If she was annoyed for whatever reason, or not even annoyed, she would come over to the bed and start hitting me whilst I was laid down in bed, half asleep. In those days we didn't have thick duvets, only a thin eiderdown, so my body wasn't protected from her hitting. She would start slowly hitting with her hand, and then end in a frenzied attack, like a crescendo, where she lost total control, hitting and punching with both hands. She even used to climb onto my bed so I could not move, pressing her horrible, fat, overweight body onto me. I had to wait until she was out of breath and stopped. She did not exercise and with being overweight she wasn't fit. I used to hope she would faint, have a heart attack or just die. Anything, just to stop her from hitting and punching me like she did. Sometimes my father would hear the screaming from her, and myself, and had to literally drag her off me. After that I was usually sobbing uncontrollably and had nowhere to escape in that bedroom. Even if I rolled on the floor, which I had tried once, I would be trapped between the bed and the other wall, giving her even more chance to thump me or even kick me, as I wouldn't be able to get up easily. I had thought of escaping out of the window but I would have to break the glass with something heavy, then throw myself out, as the window only had two small opening windows at the top, making it impossible to crawl out.

Basically I was trapped and had to endure years of this. I even wondered if this is how my father felt when he had been made to fight his brother for his parents' 'entertainment'. Trapped and nowhere to escape to – if that was the case, why didn't he stick up for me and help? He was bloody weak and daren't stick up for himself or even have an opinion. I was so annoyed with him. When each of my hitting sessions had subsided, I could never go to sleep again as I had a bunged-up nose from all the crying and a thumping headache, also pain where she had used her fists to hammer down repeatedly on my body, usually on my back so it would make me almost breathless.

I soon learned to sleep with one eye open. Hence the name of this book. I would never sleep properly again. I had to be alert and mentally prepared for the onslaught of shouting and then the hitting and thumping when I was in a vulnerable position. How could I defend myself when I was half asleep and laid horizontal? I made a promise to myself that I would never go into a deep sleep again. I had to be mentally and physically ready. Mother was also known to come into the bedroom after the first round, for a second round of hitting, it was like round two of a boxing match. There was no respite, I could never sleep again. A few times I did sleep on the floor at the far end of the bedroom, without pillows or an eiderdown. I used to put my pillows inside the bed and make them into a shape as if I was sleeping in the bed, so if she did start on the hitting routine again, she would be hitting pillows and not me. Unfortunately, every time I did this, she never came into the bedroom for another round. So I still didn't get any sleep either way as I was too cold on the floor and too anxious to sleep.

To this day I am a light sleeper and I am sure it is because of this mental and physical trauma I had to endure in that bedroom for years. Mother used to say that if I don't like it then to leave, it was 'her house and her rules' and we all had to 'do as she says whilst under her roof', all the usual old-fashioned sayings that used to be said to hurt children's feelings. I was used to it by now. I said I would leave then, even though I had nowhere to go, but anywhere – even Hessle Foreshore, or the caravan at Hornsea, was better than being in that house. I knew I could get the bus to Hornsea if I stole some money for a bus fare out of my mother's purse, but I could not find the spare caravan key. Sometimes my grandma hid a key under the caravan steps but I could not guarantee it was there. Otherwise I would have gone to the caravan and stayed there, things like food and a change of clothes were irrelevant. I just wanted to leave, go far away, feel safe and get some proper sleep.

As well as the bedroom wardrobe nightdress incidents, another ritual was happening. The spot picking and squeezing ritual. I wasn't sure how much more I could cope with everything, to be honest, but had nowhere to go and no one to tell. My mother was only intelligent in a vindictive way, and if I had reported anything to the school she would have laughed it off and put it down to my 'imagination and attention seeking'. In those days people believed the adult not the child. I knew I was trapped.

At this time I used to love gymnastics and sport at school and was fairly good at it. Unfortunately, due to not having a shower in the bathroom, and only allowed one bath per week (on a Sunday night which was also hair-wash night with Vosene shampoo), my skin used to suffer. Bearing in mind also that we had to share one face flannel between four of us, and heaven knows where else it had been on people! We had one bar of Imperial Leather or Lifebuoy soap (which is now banned in the UK!). The soap lasted for months. Unfortunately, I had greasy skin and greasy hair and kept having outbreaks of spots. If I had been allowed to get bathed more and wash my hair then I am sure this would not have been the case but that's Mother for you, telling you when you can and can't get washed or bathed, and even tut when you needed to go to the toilet. She was a control freak.

I had spots and lumps on my face and in my ears and they were painful. I used to pick them with my fingernails but it only made them bleed. My mother enjoyed pressing her sharp fingernails into my face to squeeze the spots. I used to cry out as she left 'V' marks across my cheeks, forehead and nose from her sharp, pointy shaped nails, but she enjoyed it. I decided that I would have to wash my face in the sinks in the toilet block at school, in private, numerous times a day to try and clear the spots and the grease. I did this continually but I still had the spots and greasy skin. I was getting more and more depressed as I knew that having spots meant Mother's sharp nails would be squeezing my spots and causing redness, scarring and pain. She usually did this almost surgical procedure on the settee in the back room, so it was another excuse to keep out of the same room as her so she couldn't get me.

My one saving grace was that my mother started work again for a few hours a week. 'I need some pin money,' she used to tell me. I guessed she meant money for herself as I hadn't a clue what pin money actually was, and I am sure a pack of pins would be only a few pennies. More old-fashioned sayings that didn't make sense. My father used to give her housekeeping money every Friday and left it on the mantelpiece for her. But she wanted more, as usual. One thing for certain was that she never spent it on a lot of food as Matthew and I were always flipping hungry.

Mother started work at Hick's or Hay's Bakery (I cannot remember the name for certain), which was to become McLeish Bakers. The bakery was down Boothferry Road, between Five Ways roundabout and the Hull City Football Stadium. She had to work on a Saturday morning and usually got my father to drive her there. Yes, my father had somehow managed to buy another second-hand car, which was a Humber Septre, so mother had to take advantage of this. I think the Morris Minor had gone to the scrap yard on First Lane called Winters. When father came home from dropping her off at the bakery early on Saturday morning, he would try and look after us but hadn't a clue. He actually let us watch television to keep us quiet. This consisted of Matthew and me watching 'Banana Splits' and then 'Here Come the Double Deckers', then 'Why Don't You ...?' on the television (probably repeats but we didn't care) and then father would attempt to cook us all some dinner, which was always sausages and mash. The sausages were always burned, but my mother would be home by midday and he wanted to put some dinner on the table – it was as if she'd been away for twenty-four hours, not four hours, the preparation he had to put into it with peeling and boiling the potatoes! You would think he had cooked a three-course meal.

However, one Friday night my father came home and said he had to work first thing Saturday morning, and could not look after us or cook dinner. Mother was not happy and had a drama about it all as usual. She could not take time off work either to look after us. In their limited strange wisdom they both decided that we would all get up very early on the Saturday morning. My mother and father would drive Matthew and me to the Hessle Library and then my father would drive my mother to work in Hull, en-route to his work at the post office down Lowgate in Hull. We all got up early and I remember it was winter and freezing with snow and ice on the ground and still dark. We all got into the car and I had some library tickets in my pocket in case I needed to borrow some more library books. Their idea was that we were both to stay in the library for a few hours, looking at and reading books in the children's section, and then walk home by noon when they may be then back from work.

We arrived at Hessle Town Hall where the library was based. Matthew and I both got out of the car and my father drove off without even a goodbye. It was still dark and extremely cold and my hands were freezing already and teeth chattering. The town hall building was large and old fashioned; it was where I had my previous bad experience of ballet and tap-dancing classes. We both walked to the side entrance of the building which had separate steps to the library, this had a large wooden door with the opening and closing times listed on a separate plaque. The library did not open until 9.30am and it was currently only 7.30am! Matthew and I had nowhere to go, we did not have any house keys to even walk home and give this up as a bad job. All we could do was huddle together on the cold, wet, concrete doorsteps of the library for two hours until someone came to open the doors. We did not want to sit at the front of the building as it would be a bit obvious that we had been left alone, like flaming latchkey children.

In addition to this, Hessle Police Station was next door to the town hall, and I didn't want us to get into any trouble, so we both hid away. The ballet and tap class would also be starting by about 9.00am, so people would be arriving and I didn't want to answer any questions from other parents. Eventually, still freezing cold, we were let into the library where I had to try and keep Matthew under control; obviously he got bored easily and didn't want to read any books as he was only five years old. He much preferred watching the television at home. He was running around the main library like a maniac, so I had to persuade him to stay in the children's section otherwise we would bring too much suspicion to ourselves and may be asked to leave.

I had thought of going to my grandma's house as it wasn't far away and knocking on her door, as she had a lovely open coal fire to keep warm. It was a nice idea and would be lovely to be warm, and she made lovely hot milky drinks that we never got at home. But I daren't as she would tell my mother and we would get into trouble. Also her favourite saying was 'I will knock your blocks off' or 'I will knock your heads together', which meant she literally would bang both our heads together causing headache, pain and tears. She would also try and keep us quiet by continually telling us the story of Anne Frank and the threat of being killed if she wasn't quiet during the war. That had put the fear of God into Matthew about the Germans coming to kill him. He was reluctant to talk as it was, never mind hearing the threat of being killed if you DID talk. Even though she was a batty grandma at times with her scary stories and head-knockings, she wasn't as bad as my mother. I could not risk going there as it had too many consequences and repercussions if my mother found out.

We stayed put in the library until about 11.30am sitting near the large old-fashioned bronze-coloured radiators to keep warm, and then ventured back out into the snow and ice, walking the journey back to Belvedere Road that was almost a mile. When we told my mother and father about not being let into the library until 9.30am, they didn't seem too concerned, even when I said we were both freezing cold. It was as if they did not care about us, which in reality was hurtful as they probably didn't.

It was coming up to Christmas time and my mother had put up an artificial Christmas tree in the front room – this was the room normally out of bounds, but Christmas seemed an exception for some reason. We were allowed in there between the 24th and 31st December and that was it, it was locked again. My mother had made my father put a bolt on the top of the sliding doors separating the front and back room, so we could not reach it and definitely were not allowed in there. The Christmas tree took pride of place near the window in the front room with all its baubles, tinsel and coloured lights. I think this was to show off to the neighbours that we had a lovely welcoming home and were all having such a Merry Christmas. This could not be further from the truth.

Mother's Christmas decorations were a lot to be desired. Some were made out of glass and some were silky material with horrible star patterns on them. Mother had used the top part of the wardrobe in my bedroom to store the Christmas decorations in. Heaven knows why when she could have put them all up in the loft that my father had boarded out.

Just before Christmas I decided to open the sliding door at the top of the wardrobe, thinking that my Christmas presents may be there and have a sneaky look. I had to stand on the edge of my bed and reach up and over to open the sliding door. Unfortunately, as I opened the door, the cardboard boxes that were full of decorations must have been resting against the sliding door, and literally fell out of the cupboard. The glass and brittle baubles and ornaments broke into what seemed like hundreds of pieces on my bedroom floor. There was glitter and small pieces of glass everywhere. Oh my God, Mother was going to go mad if she saw this! I carefully rewrapped the baubles in the small pieces of tissue and tissue paper that they had originally been wrapped in, then put them back in the cardboard boxes as if nothing had happened. There were no presents at the back of the cupboard that I could see, and I couldn't reach them anyway if there was. I closed the sliding door with difficulty and then tried to forget about the broken decorations.

When my mother carried the boxes downstairs ready to decorate the Christmas tree I was sat cringing. She opened the boxes and was annoyed that they were broken. She shouted over to my father to come and have a look. I just sat with a poker face trying not to react. My father told her it was the way she had packed the decorations the previous year and putting them on top of each other in the wardrobe, that's what broke them. I obviously did not correct him, and just sat quietly, silently breathing a sigh of relief.

Mother managed to find a few decorations that were not glass and therefore not broken, to put on the Christmas tree. She had to supplement the missing ornaments with chocolate Christmas decorations that were wrapped in foil and hung on the branches with gold coloured thread. Matthew and I hatched a plan. We would take the chocolates out of the foil and stuff the foil, in the same shape as the chocolates, with tissue. This was easier said than done, the shapes of the chocolates were Christmas trees and jingle bells etc. When Mother was cooking the tea we would remove a couple of the chocolates, eat them, then try and replicate the shape with tissue and rewrap it. We loved our masterplan as we could eat all the chocolates on the tree and no one would know.

Unfortunately, at Christmas time my father said to us both

that as we had been well-behaved (a bloody miracle) we could select a chocolate off the tree! We had to lie by saying that we weren't hungry and maybe tomorrow we would have one. I was worried we would get found out. So the next plan was that we would remove all the stuffed chocolates the next day and say that we had eaten them all in one go. Phew, we got away with it. We would rather be told off for eating all the chocolates at once, than being found out that we had stuffed them with tissue and already eaten them. I was getting to be a master of lying and wriggling my way out of situations.

As my father worked at the post office, there used to be a Christmas party for the children of employees at the Hull main Lowgate branch. I am not sure if the employees had to pay a contribution but I know we were forced to go. It involved getting dressed up in our best clothes (these were still old fashioned and never really fitted us), then getting a bus to Hull Paragon Station and walking to Hull New Theatre to watch the annual Christmas pantomime. Mother and Father came along, obviously in their best outfits, then after the pantomime performance we all walked to the post office in Lowgate for the children's Christmas party. The children had to sit at tables in the main canteen. Matthew and I did not know anyone. I felt really self-conscious as I was being watched by Mother and Father, who were sat on chairs at the side of the room. After the party food, which was actually quite nice and a change from the usual boring stuff at home, there was the chance to play party games. I could not be bothered so went over to my mother and father, I was told to not be so rude and was forced to sit on the floor and join in the party games. I just did not want to be there anymore. I was still wary of strangers and this room was full of people I did not know. I was out of my comfort zone and didn't like it. Of course this behaviour was an embarrassment to my parents and on the bus home I was told to be more sociable and got a long, boring lecture. Matthew was too young to be told off, but apparently I should know better. It was as if one minute I was being forced to 'shut up and sit down' like a dog, then suddenly I had to turn on a switch and was expected to be all 'happy and chatty' and playing around, like I hadn't a care in the world. Well it did not work like that for me. I knew I was an embarrassment to my parents and they would have preferred exhibitionist Carol than myself as their child.

My Christmas presents that year were a lot to be desired of from 'Father Christmas' (which I already knew did not exist) and the rest of my aunties and uncles, which I rarely saw. They consisted of Knitting Nancy – which was basically a bobbin with a hole in the middle, with four hooks on the top of it that you used to crochet and create a long string of knitting. There wasn't a great deal you could do with it. It was called French knitting and produced a long snake-like piece of crocheting. Great, I acted as if it was amazing but really I was bored from it. I also got a pom-pom making kit. I could already make pom-poms without a flipping kit. All you need is two round pieces of cardboard and some wool for heaven's sake. We got a selection box each but never allowed the chocolate ones, we always seemed to get the cheaper ones with small packets of Jelly Tots, fruit pastilles and Spangles in them.

Matthew and I also got a game to 'share', which was KerPlunk. I had now given up with the 'sharing' as I realised that Matthew somehow generally got more than me and was always the 'favourite'. I do not know what had happened to change this scenario, but suddenly I was always the 'black sheep' of the family. The only fun thing about KerPlunk was the yellow plastic pointy straws that were quite sharp at the end; I could poke them into Matthew's arm or hand and he would shout out. They never actually hurt him much, but it was fun to see his reaction.

Apparently we weren't allowed to get bikes or any outdoor toys for Christmas as Mother used to tell us 'It's winter and too cold to go outside.' That was really an excuse for not having to pay for extra toys. Obviously the other parents down the road didn't feel the same way as they were out there with their children, with their bikes and roller skates. We watched them from the front room window that we were allowed into for the one week over Christmas time.

To contradict all what Mother said about it being cold, on Boxing Day we used to have to walk to Hessle Foreshore, and it wasn't too 'cold' for that just a day later I noted. It was the most boring walk in the world, especially from Belvedere Road; it was the walking journey to hell. This was in 1973, the Humber Bridge had just recently been started, but there was nothing exciting to see yet – only Dunston's Shipyard, and further on the River Humber with just mud and stones. I hated it and used to follow behind like a lost dog with my head facing downwards. Who in their right mind would walk all that way, nearly two miles, young children in tow, to see the muddy River Humber, in winter?! They had never walked that far in their lives themselves (well my father might have on his postal round), but my mother certainly hadn't. Why put on a show on Boxing Day by getting us all dressed up and walking all that way in the freezing cold? It was beyond comprehension.

The next time my mother and father had to work at the same time, my mother decided to ask my grandma to look after us both. I think if we were to visit Hessle Library again for hours on end, then it may have aroused suspicion. My grandma meant well but hadn't a clue either. She was supposed to be looking after Matthew and me for only a few hours whilst Mother had to work at the bakery in Hull. You would have thought it was a fairly simple task to watch the children, even play with them, give them a drink of milk or juice if they whinge, that sort of normal routine.

It was spring time and Matthew and I were in the house. Grandma was right down at the bottom of the garden, near the garage, weeding and cutting the flowers. This was her idea of 'looking after us'. 'Out of sight, out of mind', was more like it. I ventured outside with a cushion in my hand, I had got it off the settee and it was a round yellow one with embroidered daisies. I was going to use it to do handstands against the wall near the back door. I loved gymnastics, headstands and handstands. I wasn't allowed to do them at school anymore, as when I was in the old Hourne area in infants school, I thought I would do a handstand against the horrible, smelly outside toilet block wall. Unfortunately, as I pushed my legs up into the air, I accidentally managed to kick another girl right in her face and hurt her. The dinner lady who was supervising us all at that time, went mad with me and sent me to stand outside some classroom door as punishment. Not that I cared about any punishment, but I did feel sorry for the girl I had kicked. It was a genuine accident.

Back at home, Matthew came outside to watch me and was playing with the wooden sweeping brush nearby and pretending to sweep the concrete ground. I did a few headstands and used the cushion under my head so as not to hurt my head on the ground, the cushion was now getting a bit dusty and dirty but I didn't care. The next thing I know, the sweeping brush was coming down onto my head and hurting me. Matthew had managed to lift it up and wallop me on the top of my head as I was standing up from a headstand. I suddenly felt quite ill and dazed, so walked into the house and upstairs to my mother's bedroom to look in her mirror on the dressing table. I could not reach any other mirrors in the house as they were all too high on the walls for me.

I felt even worse when I saw myself in the mirror, there was blood dripping onto my shoulders and splattered over my clothes. I didn't know what to do, should I call 999 for an ambulance, or go and see my grandma outside? But she was right down at the bottom of the garden and I felt really sick. I shuffled down the stairs on my bottom, in case I fainted, and then tried to walk to my grandma, who was still weeding. She saw me and got into a panic, I asked her to get some help, she said 'Oh I will call Aunty Kathleen. She will take you to hospital.' What the hell that was all about I do not know. My aunty lived in Anlaby which was only a few miles away, but she still needed to get into her car to get to Hessle, plus she had her own children to look after. It would have been quicker and easier by ambulance. Luckily, after a frantic phone call, she soon came and saw the state of me, and asked my grandma where the tea towels were. She obviously hadn't a clue, so I had to show her the tea towel drawer. She said she was going to put one on my head to try and stop the bleeding. I chose my mother's best tea towel, which had a picture of a dog printed on it. I think it was one you got free from sending off tokens from Richmond Sausages or some sausage manufacturer. It had a Bassett Hound dog picture on it. Aunty Kathleen folded it into a triangle shape and then tied it, similar to a headscarf my mother would wear, under my chin. Then we went in her car to Hull Royal Infirmary. I didn't really get on with my aunty, but she really looked after me. I felt almost comfortable and needed, and I wasn't used to it.

At the hospital I had to have quite a few stitches. My head had a huge gash on it from the impact of the sweeping brush. The nurse who was doing the stitches was comforting and saying how brave and good I was. I wasn't feeling brave; brave was surviving being hit by the Flatley sticks and not crying. Compared to that pain, the stitches on my head didn't even hurt, and when she finished I just said in a polite tone 'Is that it?' She replied yes and mentioned that I would have a sore head for a while and not to play sport at school. Also, definitely no headstands or handstands! I smiled at her and thanked her. I think she was amazed I wasn't crying or upset as I just got off the hospital bed I was on and got ready to go home.

My aunty asked if I wanted to go and see my mum at work? Of course I flaming well didn't, but what could I say? She drove to the bakery and we walked in together. At least there was safety in numbers, and I knew that nothing bad was going to happen to me if Aunty Kathleen was there. My mother acted surprised when she saw me; well I couldn't actually tell if it was surprise, shock or embarrassment to be honest. She obviously asked my aunty what had happened. They had a short conversation, then the next thing I knew I was back in her car and being driven home. I didn't want to go back home. I now wanted to stay in the warm car with my aunty as I felt safer, but I had no option. I knew I would get some snide comment from my mother later on when she came back from work, as if it was my fault, not Matthew's.

CHAPTER 10

Confliction and Restriction

Melanie and I were best friends at school and I had learned to trust her. She was still needier and fussier than me, a bit of a drama queen at time (but certainly not as dramatic as cousin Carol), but she was honest and quite caring – qualities that I liked in her. I could excuse her fussiness because of this. She must have thought I was a bit mad though as I was quite rude and ignorant in my mannerisms sometimes, but she stuck by me. I think I was only rude as I did not know any different and was angry inside from the way I was treated at home. It was nothing that Melanie had done herself; I was just always anxious and wary, especially of new situations, or the unexpected.

This was 1973 and we were now both in the same class and both loved music, especially playing the recorder. I bet we sounded horrendous playing that not very tuneful musical instrument, but we thought we sounded good and we got encouragement from a fabulous, patient music teacher at the school called Mr Chignell. We both absolutely adored him, as did most of the children at the school. He would let us do some solo recorder playing and duets. He would sometimes play the piano quietly in the background for us to follow the tunes. He was so talented that I was in awe of him. Nothing fazed him, even if we made mistakes in our musical notes, he just carried on. I think he just loved encouraging pupils with their musical skills in general. He had my utmost respect and I wished I knew more adults like him. I sometimes wished he was my father, as Mr Chignell was sensible. Unfortunately my father wasn't, and used to embarrass me by telling his stupid boring jokes that only he laughed at, and then proudly removing his false teeth at inappropriate times revealing a ugly, gummy, 'gurning face' – and he thought this was funny?! Why he couldn't be sensible and responsible was beyond me, Mr Chignell was the only real adult I could trust and respect at this time.

Melanie and I also used to love sport and gymnastics, along with quite a few other girls in the class. I wasn't really sure why I enjoyed sport as all the rest of my family were unfit and couldn't run down the garden path never mind run in a race. Maybe I had to prove I was different? Maybe it was a release for me? We had Mr Bury to help us with our gymnastics; he was a young teacher with dark hair, and used to make us laugh with his funny jokes. I remember Melanie, Jackie, Katrina and myself doing gym practice in the school assembly hall at dinner times, we all got on well together. Other boys and girls were there from different years at school, but we were all in the same class and were friends. Mr Bury was also patient and helped us learn a lot about gymnastics and the strength you needed to be a really good gymnast. He even let us play on those small trampettes, the ones like springboards, and I loved the feeling of jumping even higher and then sometimes falling onto a crashmat. Music and gymnastics were definitely my favourites, I could easily forget about all other boring school work.

The junior school were having a sports day at the school very soon, and Mr Bury was asking if anyone wanted to go onto the school field after school and do some sport practice in preparation. I, of course, said yes straightaway. I wasn't sure when it was but then he announced it was that day at about 4pm. So I followed him and went onto the school field, it had been marked out into different running lanes with that flaky white chalk. It looked really important, almost like the Olympic Games that I had once seen on television. There were quite a few other children there all waiting to practice. I threw myself into all the practice events, the obstacle race, running race, egg and spoon race, sack race and others. It was a hot June teatime and I was absolutely boiling hot from all the running, and my face was bright red! By the time I also walked home I think I had been sunburned also as my arms and neck were red and burning hot.

Mother was at home and when she saw me she went mad saying that I should have told her where I was. I said I didn't have chance as I only found out that afternoon about the sport practice. Maybe I had been told earlier but I could not remember. I could see her point, but I could hardly run home to ask her – she may have said 'no' – and then run back to the school field again to let Mr Bury know I could not come, could I? This was the time before teachers would contact parents about after school activities or clubs, so there was not a lot I could do, was there? I had had such a good time after school and was happy, but now it had now been spoilt by her shouting. You would have thought she would have been pleased if I had 'gone missing' as she would have then had a better life.

Parents were invited to the sports afternoon on the field. Melanie's mother had come to see Melanie participate in the games. Her mother was always coming to our school plays and sports events, and I was so upset that my parents never made an effort to come and see me. They had never been to any event I had been in. Melanie said it didn't matter, but I knew she was just being nice and I wished I had a mother who would come and see what I did at school and see how hard I worked, and watch the school plays, the playing in the school orchestra, and sports day. I think I was probably the only pupil that never had any encouragement from my parents. But looking back there were a few children at the school who were living at Hesslewood Orphanage. I wonder if they felt the same? I knew not to complain as they had it worse than me and had no support, through no fault of their own. Hindsight is a wonderful thing, and I wish I had shown more compassion to those children, as every day must have been lonely for them, and a lot worse than my life. I decided to do my own warm-up before the races began. In my wisdom I decided to run around the school field, obviously by the time I had done this I was shattered out; it was more like a marathon that a warm-up. Still, it got my adrenaline ready for the races. I came first in the obstacle race and second in a couple of other events, so not too bad really, considering I had used up all my energy already!

I remember the next Friday at school assembly; we all had to sit, as usual, cross-legged on the wooden, varnished, cold, shiny floor in the main school hall. Mr Phillips, the head-teacher (he was a lovely headteacher), read out the names of the children who had come first, second and third place at sports day, and we all had to go up onto the stage to be presented with our certificates and shake his hand. I felt really important going onto the stage, but unfortunately, the excitement had been marred by my mother or father not coming to the sports day to see me. I was staying packed lunch that day, so I put my certificates in my sandwich box for safekeeping, so by the time I got home they were covered in grease and other food particles. Not that my mother cared when I showed them to her. My father, on the other hand, when I showed him, was saying I should have kept them clean and was trying to clean the certificates himself with a pencil eraser and the edge of damp cloth. At least he seemed to be pleased that I had won something, the next week he actually got me a certificate or photo frame to put my 1st place obstacle race certificate in and he put it on a shelf in the back room. He seemed quite proud of me, unlike my mother who seemed annoyed that my father was paying me some attention.

Melanie's family lived in a massive detached old Victorian style house in a prime location near Swanland Road in Hessle. They had a flagpole at the front of the house which was a statement in itself! I had never seen a flag flying on it, but it didn't matter. It looked so grand. Melanie had said that her mother asked if I wanted to go for tea one night. Of course I said yes. Mother would have gladly let me go as it would save her some money by not cooking me a meal. I remember we both walked back to her house after junior school one night. When we arrived there they had a massive kitchen with a large farmhouse style table, her older sister and younger brother were also there. Food was placed in the centre of the table and you helped yourself. In our house you got a plate of food literally slammed down in front of you, like it or lump it! None of this choosing what you wanted to eat. It was like a different world, a huge house and choosing what you want to eat! It was unheard of in our household. Melanie didn't know any different, she was so lucky.

After tea we went up to Melanie's bedroom, this was also large and there was a hand basin in the corner of her room. I was so jealous, she could actually get a drink of water when she wanted to and also wash her hair in the privacy of her own bedroom. It was like a dream come true! To me it was like something you see on television, a show home. She had a massive wardrobe with beautiful clothes, unlike my Hessle 'War on Want' charity shop clothes that smelled of mothballs even after they had been washed numerous times in the twin tub.

For those who can remember, War on Want was a large charity shop at the bottom of Prestongate in Hessle. When you entered the shop it was like an Aladdin's cave of everything you could imagine from clothes, shoes, bedding, books, ornaments, toys, etc. The first thing to hit you was the smell, it smelled like a mixture of a damp house, damp dog and moth balls. The odour was musty and fusty, but in those days when you gave a donation of clothes, it was put straight on the shelves or rails, not like nowadays where they are steam cleaned to make them smell fresh. The shop wasn't by any means dirty, it was just the expanse of clothes that had probably not been washed before being donated.

The War on Want shop was massive and also had a large back room that had school uniforms for all schools in Hessle, and white school shirts (that were now more like grey, but these were the days before decent washing powder), small school skirts, trousers, blazers, ties, etc. There was even underwear! The school-wear was just laid on shelves in the shop and you had to rummage through to get the correct size, a bit like a jumble sale.

My grandma always used to go there, and would take Carol and me with her. We didn't mind it to be honest as I could look at books and she could look at dresses. My grandma just could not leave the shop empty handed and used to buy anything just for the sake of it. One of my cousins said that my grandma had a tidy up at home and donated loads of ornaments to War on Want, and then when she popped in a few weeks later, she bought them back – not realising it was what she had already donated. I am not sure if that was true, but I could certainly believe it.

I hated it when my grandma bought me clothes from there, as they smelled of mothballs, but also she would select polyester or nylon tops. She did not realise that I used to run around at school at playtimes and used to sweat like mad in those clothes. They always seemed to have big swirly patterns on like from the 1960s yet this was the 1970s. Knitted tank tops seemed to be her favourite thing to buy me for some reason, along with second-hand swimming costumes for when I had swimming lessons in the freezing cold outdoor pool at the junior school. I hated the costumes as they were either too tight or too big. I was never allowed a new swimming costume that actually fitted me.

Melanie wasn't judgemental and I did wonder what she saw in me as I didn't have nice long hair like she did, or nice clothes that actually fitted me like hers did. Besides the stigma of War on Want, my mother used to cut my hair, so it always looked like I had been dragged through a hedge backwards. She bought a cheap haircutting contraption to save money, advertised on the television as 'The Hair Magician'. Take it from me; there was nothing magic about this item. It should have been called 'The Hair Miracle' as it was a bloody miracle you even had any hair left after using it. It consisted of a comb with a sharp razor blade inside it. The idea was to be able to comb your hair and cut it at the same time. The theory being that as you pulled the comb and razor blade downwards through your hair, it would look nice and layered. This obviously did not work, as when Mother used it and dragged it down my hair, it either pulled my hair out at the roots or just pulled at my hair in general, cutting random clumps of hair along the way. The layers were not consistent, and it was bloody painful. Matthew was the best candidate for this as he had a basin cut, cut by mother with the kitchen scissors, then an attempted layer cut by using the combination of the comb and sharp razor blade. It was torture. Whoever invented that needed shooting (along with person who invented the Flatley dryer!). Melanie had lovely long, honey blonde, straight-styled hair and I reckoned she went to a proper hairdresser, unlike me.

When I got back home from Melanie's I was excited. I mentioned to my mother that Melanie had a hand wash basin in her bedroom and it was really cool. My father was in the room and piped up that he could easily fit one into my bedroom if I wanted. My bedroom was next to the bathroom, so all it needed was an extra pipe fitting from the bathroom, and a sink. He said it would save washing my hair in the bath.

Currently I was using a rubber hose attachment that you put onto the bath taps and the water got too hot and burned your head. In addition I would have more privacy and not use the only bathroom as much. I was ecstatic at this news and it seemed like my father and myself had made a good plan and even he looked hopeful and smiling. However, as soon as he said it my mother stated abruptly 'No, she's not having that in her bedroom, who the hell does she think she is, the Queen?!' So that was that idea or suggestion scuppered. My father knew it was no use arguing with her, as his life would be hell. He did say to me later on that night that he thought it was unfair as it would be an easy thing to install, but when mother had spoken, that was it. He was still being weak and wasn't allowed his opinion about anything. A bit like Matthew and myself – not allowed a voice or opinion. I would have to dream about having a sink in the bedroom then, and live with what my mother would call my 'greasy, rats' tails hair'.

Matthew and I came home one afternoon after school and there were strangers in the house that apparently were my mother's cousins who lived nearby in Willerby. They had bought with them a black Cairn terrier puppy that my mother had bought. What the hell? Apparently they had already got a Cairn terrier and it had had a litter of puppies and my mother (not wanting to miss out and trying to give a good impression) said that she would have one. This was the first I had heard of this in my life! So they put this black fluff ball on the floor in the back room and it promptly had a wee on the carpet. Mother was fussing about in the kitchen trying to find a cloth to wipe it up, her cousins left her to it and went. They were probably relieved to get rid of the dog as it was the last one in the litter to go, I was told later on. Why the hell have we got a dog when she's stressed with two children, never mind a dog? After all, she had got rid of Mitzi when I was young as she couldn't cope, none of it made any sense.

Mother had to name the new dog herself as we weren't allowed to, so had no say in it. She named it Dinky, which was a bit of an understatement as when it grew full size it wasn't exactly dinky in size, he was chunky. Dinky had black fur with a white stripe under his tail. He was quite cute and Matthew and I loved him, he used to follow us up and down the garden path and watch us play on the swings. If we left him alone he was okay, he just walked around and was either asleep near the front door where it was warm in the sun, although he was prone to chewing the mail, or he would be in the garden. Once, when he was bored and alone in the kitchen, he did jump from the kitchen bin and onto the work surfaces nibbling at things as he went along, even the soap. He was a character and frustrated Mother.

However, the back garden wasn't totally secure and he would try and dig himself a hole underneath any gap in the fence panels to escape. My mother, in her wisdom, had an idea of putting Dinky on his dog harness and a lead, then making a string loop and fastening it over the long washing line. This enabled Dinky to walk up and down the garden on his harness but as it was attached to the washing line he couldn't go onto the side of the garden near the fences and begin digging holes, but he did still have some garden to walk up and down in. The other issue was that when he got to the end of the washing line pole, he would go round and round it and unwittingly wrap his lead and string around the pole, like a maypole, and then begin barking as he couldn't move any further! So he had to be rescued and unravelled every now and again. I could tell Mother was losing her patience with Dinky, first by him digging holes in the garden and digging up flowers, secondly by him being stuck at the end of the washing line pole and barking so the neighbours could hear. It wasn't Dinky's fault, it was hers. Why they just didn't put better fencing or chicken wire across the adjoining gardens I will never know. Also Mother could not hang any washing out when Dinky was attached to the washing line! She hadn't thought of that had she? She hadn't a clue about the practical side of things.

One person I could talk to was Doreen, our next-door neighbour, but I kept conversations a bit vague and knew not to elaborate too much, Mother might have been listening from the kitchen window. She once baked some scones and asked if Matthew and I wanted to come and see her and have some of her baking. Of course we said yes, but had to ask Mother. Surprisingly, she agreed. We had an adjoining gate at the side of the garden fence, so we just unbolted this and went into her garden and entered her house. She had put butter on the warm scones and they were delicious. Looking back I think she must have heard the usual shouting and screaming from Mother, and the crying from us and felt sorry for us. She probably realised how much weight we were losing and baked out of kindness. I will never know, but I was grateful either way.

I also loved sewing. This was the 1970s when patchwork quilts were trendy and people began making them by hand-sewing different materials together. I decided to make a quilt out of hexagon shapes. The most common shapes were squares as it was easier, but for some reason I wanted hexagons. I would sit in my bedroom and cut out numerous hexagon templates, all the same size, onto cardboard or newspaper. Then cover them with different fabrics and after tacking them, would sew them together by hand.

Sometimes on a Saturday I used to visit the Remnant Shop in Hessle, that was situated down a long passageway next to Skeltons Bakery on Hessle Square. I had been here a couple of times with my mother on the rare occasions she took me to the shops in Hessle.

The shop had a brown-framed glass door leading into the shop, and inside it was nice, quiet and calming, which I liked. It sold items such as rolls of material, cottons and I remember looking at the masses of Butterick patterns to make your own dresses and skirts etc. I wished I could buy a pattern to try it out but knew my mother would not give me the money for one, so I used to look through the plastic catalogue pages of them almost in awe of the different styles and shapes you could make. The rolls of material were stacked up on shelves and I enjoyed feeling the textures and looking at the designs. How I wished I could make a nice top and not have to make do with War on Want second-hand clothes.

There was an off-cut container where they put the material in that was at the end of a roll and a bit scraggy. I would rummage through this and try and find some cheap off-cuts for my patchwork quilt with my limited pocket or birthday money. After a few times of popping into the shop, one of the ladies recognised me and said they had acquired a carrier bag full of off-cuts and they were saving it for another girl that also used to come in doing patchwork, but she hadn't been in for a while. She asked if I wanted it. I could not believe it, something so small and it meant so much to be actually given something for free. I think I mumbled 'thank you', not because I was ungrateful, but because I was in shock that someone was actually being nice to me.

I told her I was making a patchwork quilt and I think she probably felt sorry for me, or maybe just genuinely wanted to encourage my sewing skills. I almost ran home with that carrier bag held close to me, I could not wait to open it to see the materials and feel the textures. This was better than Christmas.

When I got home I went up to my bedroom to lay out all the material pieces. All the different colours, patterns, textures, smells and styles of material intrigued me and I couldn't wait to begin to cut the material into hexagons. Eventually I would sew the pieces together to make a trendy quilt cover and then would sew this onto the thin quilt that I had on my bed that was now ripped, probably from Mother's fists trying to pound through it to hurt me even more. It would cover the rips and make it look modern, rather than the pink, old-fashioned flowery design that was on there currently. To be honest the quilt was so thin it wasn't worth putting it on the bed as each night I was freezing in that room. But I had it all planned out in my head: what I was going to do and the way to do it, all sewn by hand.

This kept me busy for hours at a time over the weekends. I didn't need to go downstairs to speak to anyone, I was just up in my room, hand-sewing. At least I was doing something productive and had an end goal. I was called ignorant by mother, but I didn't care. At least I was out of the way, or rather out of HER way, 'out of sight – out of mind' she used to quote, well I now agreed! If I could have put a lock on the bedroom door I would have, just to keep Mother out and have peace and quiet. Even hearing her stomping, heavy footsteps coming up the stairs frightened me, and my heart would beat faster. At least if I had a lock on the door I could keep her out and not be as nervy. I knew that I wouldn't be allowed one.

By this time, my father had done a lot of DIY in the house at the weekends, which was not all brilliant quality but it had saved Mother some money, and now he decided to build himself a train layout in the loft. The loft was now fully boarded out with thin wooden panels on the inside of the loft roof and then chipboard on the floor. He also cut out a larger loft hatch to get these panels into the loft, and installed some wooden loft ladders. These were a danger in themselves. The problem was that if you were in the loft and didn't look down, you could easily fall through the large loft hatch and land a few metres down onto the landing, probably breaking a limb on the fall down! Plus if the loft hatch hadn't been put back up properly by the small spring catch, the hatch would just spring open and the heavy wooden ladders would fall down themselves, possibly on someone's head underneath the hatch.

This was now my father's retreat, the loft. He wasn't usually at work at weekends now, so would spend all his time building a train layout that was about three and a half feet off the floor of the loft and weaved around the whole loft. It also got him out of the way of Mother, I realised. He spent years doing that loft and the train layout, as a so-called hobby and an escape. He would still go and visit his mother in Hull on a Sunday morning now and again, and then come back and go into the loft. It was boiling hot up there as there was no ventilation, and even warmer since being boarded out, but he didn't seem to care, it was his escape from the real-life dramas of Mother.

My back bedroom, on the other hand, was dark and

freezing cold as it never got any sun through the windows to warm it up. Mother's theory about having the hot water tank cupboard in the room keeping me warm was a load of rubbish. When we had central heating installed, I wasn't even allowed a radiator in my bedroom. My bedroom was the only room in the house with no central heating. I would spend the night with my teeth chattering and body shivering as I was so cold. I would put on socks and cardigans as being so cold would wake me up. It was a bit like being in the caravan at Hornsea. In fact I think the caravan probably had better insulation!

I had now made some friends down Belvedere Road. They were not needy or show-offs like some girls I had met previously, and we got on well. Julie was my age and lived about ten doors down the road to myself, she went to Penshurst school and had an older sister and younger brother. Julie was, and still is, very petite and quietly spoke. Alison lived across the road and was a year older than me. She had two older siblings and was quite a confident person. We would listen and believe anything she said as she was older and wiser than us. Suzanne was a year younger than me; she lived near the top of the street and had a younger brother and even younger sister who was only about four years old. The whole family had just moved from Cyprus as I think her father was in the Forces there. Suzanne talked really quietly and was attractive with long blonde hair and a slim figure. All three had qualities that I admired. Out of them all I was the 'loose cannon' in the group and could be abrupt, not meaning to be, but I couldn't help myself. I used to secretly cringe after some of the things I had said to them. I would go over and over my comments in my head, when I was in bed. I certainly did not want to end up like Mother, criticising people and being nasty. I would try really hard not to let this happen.

We girls, we had a sort of routine. One of us would sit on our front garden wall and then the others would see and come out to join everyone else. It was our way of saying we needed to talk or play. As our (or rather my Mother's) wall was viewable to all the others from their windows. They would linger around outside our house in the street. When we did come together we would just talk, play Block, or just do our own gymnastic shows on the small bit of grass in the street at the front of the house. We never argued, disrespected anyone who was passing by, or caused any trouble. These girls were a good, calming influence on me.

Mother knew this and just had to think of ways to interfere and upset everyone. She said she went to school with Julie's mother, so I asked why she didn't go and speak to her then? She couldn't answer that, so I wasn't sure if there was any animosity between them both. It was a bit strange as Julie's mother was always polite to me. Also my father made friends with Julie's father, Brian, and they both had an interest in steam trains. Again, much to Mother's annoyance and jealousy.

Alison and Suzanne were also the brunt of my mother's opinions. They both lived in council houses near the top of the street. The houses were much bigger than ours and backed onto an open field, so were really private with huge back gardens. Ours was a mid-terrace house with a small front paved garden and a narrow back garden. Mother just had to have her opinion about them living in a council house. I said that I thought Suzanne's family had come from Cyprus and had nowhere to live in England, so that is why they were given a council house. My mother was still trying to grasp at straws and said that I should be grateful that I lived in a house that she paid for, and not a council house. I knew she was lying as it was actually my father who paid for it as he worked full-time, she didn't. To me, it didn't matter where they came from or where they lived. I didn't really understand the concept of what a 'council house' meant anyway, I was only nine years old. They were my friends, they never hurt me, we got on well and I respected them. My mother was such a snob, yet she had no friends. I was confused. She now seemed to want to turn my friends against me so I would become a loner and she would have more control over me. I personally would have swapped to live in one of their houses any day, as they were massive – I didn't understand Mother's logic at all. If she was so much of a snob, then why buy a house down a street with council houses?

One afternoon, after school, I sat on our front brick wall to see if anyone would come out to join me. The girls all came out and we were laughing and talking together sat on the wall. My mother must have been in the front room, with the window open, listening to us. She was obviously allowed in the front room – we weren't. She knocked loudly on the front room window and beckoned for me to come inside the house. I begrudgingly did so. When I got in the house she gave me a barrage of abuse, almost spitting in my face, saying that she didn't see why everyone had to sit on HER wall when they had their own walls to sit on. I said it was because our wall was in the middle of the street and we could all see each other and join in. She told me to tell them to move away from her wall and never sit on it again. I held back the tears, she was causing friction between my friends now, and I hated her interfering. We were doing no harm, just talking, but even that annoyed her. I was dreading telling Julie, Alison and Suzanne this, and felt foolish and an idiot, almost like 'Mother's puppet'.

I felt physically sick but went back outside and into the

street. Alison asked if I was okay. I knew I was being used as a go-between and I hated it. I said to Julie, Alison and Suzanne that my mother wanted us to move away from the wall. I kept it vague deliberately. They looked confused but just said 'Okay, we will sit on the grass then.' I was grateful it never came to an argument between us, which is what Mother had originally wanted. They must have thought I was bloody crazy, a flaming nutcase, but these three friends stuck by me, whatever Mother made me do to try and destroy our friendship. Luckily her plan never worked, but that was how vindictive and petty she was. In fact, these girls are still my friends forty-five years later – so sorry Mother, your plan backfired big time!

Julie's house was a similar style to ours but not quite as modern, but who cared? Only my mother. I was fascinated by a wooden bar her father had that was in the shape of a ship, that took pride of place near the window in their front room. It had lots of full and half-opened bottles of spirits and mixers, along with loads of different size glasses, especially the Babycham glasses. I was always fascinated by the yellow liquid in the Advocaat bottle and wondered what was really in it. I could imagine Julie's father, Brian, smiling and serving drinks behind his own personal bar at Christmas time to his family and guests. He had a rounded, portly figure and had his hair slicked back with Brylcreem. He was always polite to me and seemed happy. When I visited Julie, the house was always full of chattering but no shouting. Our house was always a bloody war zone, with hitting, shouting and then crying, we had no laughter, everything was serious or we had to tread on eggshells so we didn't upset Mother.

I remember Julie inviting me round to her house for a party. I think it was her sister's party, she was a year older than Julie and quite mature for her age. Julie's mother had baked and was taking warm food out of the oven. It was delicious. She had baked vol-au-vents and I was mesmerised by the different food that I had never seen before in my sheltered life. Julie was helping and I could not help but feel a bit envious of their family life. Julie's father called Julie 'love' such as, 'Can you just get me the salt please, love?' Maybe this was how families were supposed to be? I did not know. Their house just seemed full of affection and respect for each other.

When I got home I told my mother about the bar that was in the shape of a ship in Julie's front room. She said it was ridiculous and had seen it through their front window when she had walked by the house. I went on to say it had Babycham glasses and cherries on sticks etc. and was like a real pub. Instead of asking if I had a good time at the party, she dismissed my conversation. I didn't even get to tell her I had eaten vol-au-vents. She was probably jealous anyway.

Our front room glass doors were still bolted so I couldn't see much of the outside world. I had to sneak into my mother's front bedroom and walk on tiptoes quietly, to see if my friends were waiting for me in the street. Our small back downstairs room just looked out onto a white tall breezeblock construction adjoining wall, and then the narrow garden. There wasn't much room in the back room as there was a settee and chair, an oversized round table with four chairs (that my mother ordered in the wrong size from Willis Ludlow), a cupboard for coats and an old-fashioned 1960s tall sideboard with a drop-down door. Inside this sideboard there was a bottle of sweet sherry, Captain Morgan's dark rum and a can of Mackeson stout. We were not allowed to go into this cupboard. There were also four small sherry glasses inside it, and when the door was opened it had a woody smell, probably from the two cigars that were also there for 'special occasions'. The sideboard was only opened about twice a year and that was at Christmas. What a waste of space. At least Julie's father had an open bar and used it most weeks by the look of it, and he was happy! I really couldn't believe the difference in a house styles and atmosphere just a few doors away. I knew where I would rather be living.

At the other side of Hessle, my grandma had now decided to become a 'fully-fledged' Jehovah's Witness! She now didn't celebrate Christmas or birthdays, but she still gave Matthew and I Christmas presents, although they would be wrapped up in coloured crepe paper that looked like it may have been used as a tablecloth previously. She daren't use Christmas wrapping paper as she used to as it would be a sin. I didn't mind, it's the thought that counts, plus she had other grandchildren to buy for. It made me laugh as although she didn't believe in Christmas, she always went to my aunty's house (who was not a Jehovah's Witness) for this celebration in the middle of December, and didn't return back home until the end of January.

I did not mind being at Grandma's house, as I felt I could move about a bit more freely and at least all Matthew and I got was our heads banged together, no sticks, not much hitting and definitely no spot-squeezing. She had dogs so they were a welcome distraction. Her house had French doors that went out onto an extremely neat and tidy cottage-style garden with nice smelling flowers. It was a medium-sized garden with a massive work shed, presumably this was my grandad's. Also a wooden tram seat from Hull tramway was situated in the garden, with a reversible back rest that we loved sitting on. It is probably worth a few pounds nowadays and a collectable item!

If Carol was there then we could now do almost anything and not get told off. We were allowed to make rose water by putting crushed rose petals, picked from grandma's best roses, into a jam jar and adding water to supposedly make a sort of perfume. My grandma always had old jam jars in her shed. We would also try to make butter by putting the cream from the top of milk bottles in a jar and we just kept shaking the jar until it made a thick butter consistency – that was the theory anyway. To be honest it was more like curdled milk, but it kept us busy for quite a while, competing with each other as to who could make the quickest butter. My grandma always had ideas to keep us occupied, unlike Mother. We once tore some individual sheets of toilet paper, then folded each piece into a concertina sort of fold, then got some cotton from grandma's armadillo sewing basket, and tied it in the middle to make our own pretend butterflies. My grandma had nice soft toilet paper with patterns on them, usually flower prints. We never had such luxury in our house. Mother put one toilet roll out at a time in our bathroom and the rest was kept under the sink downstairs. I am sure she did this out of spite, but then who knows? Sometimes when under stress, you begin to doubt people's motives. As Carol and I were getting older, we seemed to be getting along better together. She did still get on my nerves sometimes with her showing off and her horrendous singing, especially continually singing 'Millie, Molly, Mandy – sweet as sugar candy', I could have easily slapped her but managed to restrain myself. If I hear that song ever again I swear I will not be responsible for my actions!

One thing that Carol did hate immensely was my grandma's sewing basket. This was kept in her massive expensive and heavy wooden sideboard, which was full of old photographs of my grandma and grandad, bottles of alcohol, cut out newspaper articles, and other miscellaneous bits and pieces she had acquired throughout the years. The sewing basket was an armadillo and I was fascinated with it.

Obviously it was dead and hollowed out. I presume my grandad had bought it from abroad many years previously. Hopefully the armadillo had died of natural causes (I would like to think) and was lined with silky material and now used as a sewing basket, with needles and cottons. I was mesmerised by its black wiry hair still on its shell, and its tail was curled over and used as the basket handle. Nearly everyone else hated it, but I loved it; it was so different and unusual and I was determined to see if I could have it.

My grandma sometimes meant well, but I could tell that her favourites were all her other grandchildren, not Matthew and I. We were definitely last in the ranking order. I never really knew why, but put it down to grandma hating my mother. I would never ever know the full family history of it all.

CHAPTER 11

Aggression and Depression

I was now ten years old and reaching puberty. Along with all the other bodily changes that were happening was also my greasy skin and hair, which unfortunately seemed to be getting worse. I had spots similar to acne on my face and also across my shoulders. I also had boils on my face and in my ears, they were really painful and sometimes made my eyes puff up and swell. My mother enjoyed other people's unfortunate circumstances and was one of those people that enjoyed causing pain to others. She was always squeezing spots on my father's face, well it was actually a cyst near his ear that needed to be surgically removed, but she didn't care. She would squeeze it daily and it just became more and more infected. Why he did not go to the doctors surgery for a proper medical diagnosis is beyond me.

We had now progressed from Mother stabbing her finger nails into my face to squeeze the spots, to her new hairgrip method. Then there was the notorious kitchen stool, it had a brown sticky-back plastic-coated seat and was short, at about two feet high, and had four white metal legs. It was always pushed to the side of the wall in the kitchen, ready for action. Matthew and I nicknamed it the 'spot stool', as when my mother called me into the kitchen nine times out of ten it was for me to sit on the 'spot stool'. She would forcibly sit me on it, and then get a hairgrip and squeeze my spots on my face with the hairgrip rounded end, until my spot popped or bled. If the hairgrip didn't dig deep enough then she would use her fingernails instead which were always cut in a triangular shape with a point at the end, so much sharper and more painful.

Consequently, I ended up with small V shaped marks on my face for hours afterwards where she had pressed her fingernails deep and hard into my face. I also got scarring. I used to be screaming and crying, sometimes to an extent of sobbing so much my bottom lip would be trembling and I couldn't control it. It wasn't just one spot she would focus on, it was many spots at the same time. She would close the kitchen door whilst this was being done and Matthew would sometimes open the door to see what was happening and start laughing. He was only young about six or seven years old, so did not really understand, and he was at the age of thinking it was hilarious. Mother always shouted at him to shut the door whilst she carried on.

I remember once that I had a spot in my ear. Mother noticed it too. She made me kneel on the kitchen floor and put my head to one side on the spot stool seat so she could see the spot more easily. It was like a surgical procedure was about to take place and I felt physically sick. She was stood above me with her hairgrip in hand ready to pounce. As she pressed down hard, the boil, or spot, in my ear, exploded into her face with force of the hair grip. From inside my ear there was a loud 'crack' noise, she screamed and pushed me onto floor as if it was my fault! 'It's the badness coming out of you,' Mother would shout. 'YOU are full of BADNESS!' I had to then pick myself off the floor and endure round 2 of the spot-squeezing sessions. This routine with the spots was to continue every few days, for years, usually after tea time or during weekend, and I hated it. It made me ill with the pain. My father used to come into the kitchen to tell Mother to leave me alone, but she would only tell him to 'shut up' and close the door, and then do her stupid tutting noise. Again, a weak man, who should have listened to his children. I bet Doreen heard all of this from her adjoining kitchen and wondered what the hell was going on. It was like World War Three had broken out most days in that house with the shouting, crying and hitting. I wished it would end soon.

My Aunty Kathleen had two children, Sally and Lisa. I used to see them at my grandma's house sometimes and we would play together. We got on together okay. Lisa was a couple of years younger than me, and she had almost white porcelain skin (like a doll's), with no blemishes or grease. I used to wonder how her skin was so clear, I was almost mesmerised by it. She looked beautiful with her clear skin and long dark hair, and there I was with my greasy skin and hair – which had been cut into so-called layers by the razor comb. I never used to get along with my Aunty Kathleen, but since the sweeping brush head injury incident I now respected her and her patience. She told my mother that my spots and boils looked 'angry'. In fairness to her, that was a polite way of her saying they were looking painful and hurting me (which they were!). She asked me if they hurt me and I said yes. She then turned to my mother and asked about going to the doctors for some cream or medicine. I could see from my mother's face that she was not happy at having to make the effort of making an appointment, and then taking me to the doctors. She would not have been happy if my spots actually healed as she would not be able to use her 'spot stool' as much. I wasn't bothered anymore; I was used to the pain of the spots and boils.

I did not want to go as Mother would only embarrass me at the doctors with her stupid questions and pitiful looks and would make out that I was being 'rude'. I knew her mind games. I didn't want to be punished when I got out of the doctors. However, I do remember going once to the doctors and then Boots the chemist to get a small bottle of white liquid to put on my spots, but all that did was dry them up. Still, it wasn't as painful as what I thought I would try at home as a home-remedy for my spots.

I was desperate to get rid of my spots, acne and the so-called 'badness coming out of me' (as Mother kept reminding me) and not have to sit on the spot stool anymore to endure even more pain. Therefore, I washed my face constantly with Dettol that was in the bathroom cabinet at home. I had seen on the television adverts that it killed germs, the smell and sting of it was almost enjoyable, whereas the smell of TCP was unbearable on my skin and almost made me sick. My father used that on his so-called spot or cyst near his ear and you could seriously smell him even before he came into the room. I have never bought TCP and never will do! I also tried toilet bleach but had to wash it off quickly in less than a minute, as it seemed to burn me quickly, and was quite slimy and gel like with a really strong smell that I didn't like. Maybe it was because we shared one flannel and one towel between all four of us for a week that caused spots. Mother didn't think of that.

I used to wash my hair in the hand basin, or over the bath, during the week, but Mother complained, saying I had splashed water all over the floor, it was like she now enjoyed seeing me look scruffy with greasy hair and spots. Even if I used the shower hose attachment on the bath taps to wash my hair over the bath, she would complain about the water and the rubber hose melting on the hot water tap. I could not win. I didn't ask for much, I only wanted to be clean and smell nice.

Doreen, our neighbour, was always being kind to Matthew and myself. To be honest she probably still felt sorry for us. At Easter she bought us both an Easter egg from Thornton's

Chocolates that had our names iced on them. I could not believe it. I had never seen anything like it in my life – a large chocolate egg with my name on it. She had gone to all that trouble and expense for us two. Matthew was too young to realise this but I wasn't, and I really respected Doreen. Mother used to say that Easter eggs were a waste of money, but this was just an excuse not to buy us both one. She used to say that sweets are bad for you and that is why I had spots from too much chocolate. Well I didn't know where this chocolate was from then, as she never bought us any.

The Easter egg from Doreen was like a gift from heaven. She will never know how much we both appreciated it. I took mine upstairs and ate most of it. I didn't care if you were supposed to eat Easter eggs on Easter Sunday – according to my mother. I knew by the Sunday anything could have happened, such as an argument, and it could be taken off me. I was used to eating quickly now when I got food, and also told Matthew to do this. The number of times Mother had ranted and caused an argument at the dinner table when we had sat down to eat, and then taken our food away from us, or hit us so we would run upstairs and leave our food on the table for her to finish or throw away. I learned to eat like I was a bloody starving feral cat! I wasn't religious: that chocolate Easter egg WOULD be stuffed into my mouth in less than half an hour regardless of which day Easter was.

Matthew and I did, however, find out accidentally that Mother had a secret stash of sweets and chocolates hidden behind the green dralon settee in the front room, for her only. She left the bolted doors open once and we found them! She used to pack us off to bed and then start eating sweets herself – the thought of sharing her sweets never entered her head. One rule for her, and one for us. When she did put a pack of biscuits in the cupboard and we would reluctantly ask for one, the answers from her would be 'It's nearly tea time, you will spoil your tea.' Or, 'You have just had your tea, you can't STILL be hungry.' So whichever way, there was always an excuse not to treat us or even give us a biscuit, never mind any sweets.

This had an effect on my eating habits and I began to binge eat, as I never knew when I would be able to have food again. Even having tea at the table was a drama. Mother would cook tea and by the time she had finished cooking in the kitchen she would be huffing and puffing and in a mood. She would slam a plate of food down in front of us and call us both lazy, then cause an argument and send us both to bed, so we never got much, maybe a mouthful, to eat. If I ate quickly she would tell me off and call me greedy, but I could cope with that, at least I had eaten something rather than nothing. The usual argument was from Matthew saying that I had more on my plate than he did, Mother shouting and then saying 'You both don't deserve any food, this will teach you,' and throwing the food (our tea!) straight into the kitchen bin. Even now I have an eating issue and will sometimes wolf my food down like no one has even seen before! If I hadn't been to Melanie's house for my tea I would have thought this was normal family behaviour at the table. Melanie's family were quiet and respectful in comparison.

One morning during our walk to school, Matthew told me that someone was bullying him. He didn't know why he was being bullied, but I suspected it was as he was a bit of a strange-looking child at this time, huge blue staring eyes, almost froglike. Plus he sometimes walked with his backside stuck out – which probably was a posture or spinal medical problem, but Mother wouldn't think of this and seek any treatment for him. In addition Matthew also had long legs but every pair of trousers he had were worn half-mast, courtesy of War on Want and my mother. So there was nothing he could have done about any of these situations. Surely this didn't warrant being bullied though? If these were the actual bullying reasons? I didn't know. The word 'bullying' sent me into a defence mode on behalf of Matthew. This was like showing a red rag to a bull, and I asked Matthew who the bully was. It was someone in Matthew's year at school called Darren. I had always hated the name 'Darren' anyway, I don't know why, so that made it even more personal to me.

The next time Matthew and I were walking to school together he pointed Darren out to me. I was in the junior school, that was in a different block to the infant school. I waited outside the infant school driveway until it was a bit quieter and called him over. He obliged and came over, not knowing the implications of his actions. I went berserk telling him how bullying is wrong, he didn't seem bothered. *'I'll give you something to be bothered about,'* I thought, I got hold of his blonde hair and swung him around by it, a bit like it was a hammer throwing competition at the Olympic Games. I was spinning him around and even I felt dizzy! I eventually let go of his hair and he fell to the ground in a crumpled heap.

My fists and fingernails were full of his blonde hair that I had pulled out from the momentum of the spinning. Eventually word got back to the junior school and I was told off by my class teacher in class three, Mr Pyle. Obviously Darren had gone crying to his mother and they knew who I was. I did not care, it was worth it, plus Matthew never got bullied by him again, so my tactic worked. To this day I do not know how my mother never found out, but Matthew still remembers this and thought I was some kind of child possessed by the devil, swinging a person around by their hair! I told him to harden up and stick up to the bullies if it happened again – whatever the consequences.

I thought Mr Pyle was a difficult class teacher and could never really relax in his class. I am not sure if I just felt embarrassed as he was a male as I had nothing to say, or why I even felt that way. Every Monday morning we had to do a diary of what we did over the weekend. Most weekends I spent upstairs in my room sewing or just reading books, so I had nothing at all to put in my diary. If it was a weekend of Mother shouting and walking out, I never mentioned that either as I knew it would get me into trouble. One day during the week, Mr Pyle asked me to stay behind and asked me about my school diary. I had written one paragraph only – 'I did not do a lot over the weekend but Doreen my neighbour saw me in the garden and gave me a pack of Jelly Tots, they were nice.' I knew I had let my guard down. It was a Monday morning when I wrote that and I must have been shattered out from the weekend of either being hit or mentally tortured. I should have made something up at least, I had to be more careful in the future.

Mr Pyle sat me down at his teacher's desk at the front of the classroom when everyone else had gone and said to me that I MUST have done something else over the weekend, as well as speak to my neighbour who gave me some sweets. I told him that I didn't, but he kept pressing me to expand more on my weekend. I could not think quick enough and he was watching me as I was going more and more red in the face from embarrassment and I was trying not to release a little tear – that would show weakness and that I had lied. Then heaven help the repercussions if that got back to Mother. He eventually said I could leave the room.

I hated Mr Pyle for trying to catch me out, but looking back maybe he was also concerned about me, I could not tell. From then on I decided that each Monday in my diary I would lie and say that I had had a wonderful weekend, consisting of going shopping down Hessle Road in Hull with Mother on a Saturday, and visiting my family on a Sunday and other things that normal people do. I used to look at the other children's diaries when they were writing to get some ideas of what a normal family did. I had to be 'one step ahead' now. It seemed they did things such as going to the park, riding their bikes, seeing their grandma and grandad, walking the dog with their mother and father, and having picnics. I would copy bits from their diaries – that would get him off my back for a while. I learned to be a good liar, but hated it as sometimes Mr Pyle would ask us to stand up in class individually and read our diary out loud. I should have been an author and actress at an early age, as I managed to speak and bluff my way through a load of lies. I had to do it to cover up the reality of my supressed life.

I was still good friends with Melanie and we tried to sit together as much as we could in class. I remember I was just messing around in the class and for some random reason Melanie and I were looking at different coloured felt tip pens. I thought somehow it would be a good idea to poke her with a blue felt tip pen on her sleeve and see if the colour would run on her blue dress. So stupid, I know, but sometimes I did things for attention or if I was bored, just to get a reaction. Well she went a bit mad and showed Mr Pyle, he told her to sit down and he could not see any ink mark on her dress. When she got home she told her mother, who (unknown to Melanie and me at the time) admired Mr Pyle and used to take food and gifts to him. So now this so-called small ink mark on Melanie's dress was an ideal opportunity for her mother to visit him after school and 'discuss' this with him, and to complain about me! I had now given her a reason to visit him – all at my expense. Mind you Melanie and I did laugh about this many years later when we both found out that she had a crush on Mr Pyle.

The follow-on from this now was that Mr Pyle told me off, even though initially he said he could not see any ink mark, and then said he had to tell my mother. I was absolutely frantic. Mother would go mental with me and hit me, I knew it. Because I had now made my weekend diary to be all happy families and sweetness and light, I could not now admit to him that I lied and actually did spend all the time in my bedroom keeping out of Mother's way. I wanted to beg him not to tell Mother as I was getting more and more anxious each day thinking of the outcome.

Every night I went home from school I wondered if Mother had been told about the incident. My palpitations were getting worse and I sometimes thought I would die. I soon knew when she had been told as she laid into me as soon as I opened the front door, and I had a barrage of verbal abuse and saying that she was ashamed of me – well that was nothing new anyway. I was sent to my bedroom, but I was going up there anyway so it was no real punishment. I was expecting a lot worse.

In Mr Pyle's class we had a class gerbil that lived in the cage at the back of the classroom. We each took it in turns to feed it every day and Mr Pyle supervised. Over the weekends we had a rota and each weekend a pupil could take the gerbil home in its cage, feed it and look after it then bring it back to school on Monday morning. When it came to my turn I was so excited, I had been waiting so long for this weekend. I carried it home in its cage carefully trying not to swing it around too much. I kept it in the cage and put it on the kitchen worktop and sat on the spot stool and just watched it through the cage bars for hours. I did notice that it had only one eye but that didn't bother me. I had some food to give it from Mr Pyle, so I placed that in the cage also. I loved watching it scamper around with its food. I watched it for most of the day on Saturday.

On the Sunday morning I knew my father would get up early and, as usual, I heard Radio Humberside blaring out loud in the bathroom and heard him go downstairs. Bearing in mind I never usually went downstairs, and tried to avoid even eating, I had to make an exception this weekend to feed the gerbil his breakfast. I walked through the back room and into the kitchen to see an empty cage. Where was he?! Had he escaped?! However, the cage was empty of items such as a food bowl and water. My father was on the settee having his breakfast and said that the gerbil had died overnight and he had just buried him in the garden. This all sounded a bit strange to me and I asked to see the gerbil, but he would not tell me where he had been buried.

I was in shock and ran back upstairs to my room to recover from this trauma. What had happened to the gerbil overnight, and more importantly how the hell was I going to go back to school on Monday morning with an empty cage? Later in the day I went downstairs and I asked my father if he would come to school with me on Monday morning and tell Mr Pyle that I did not kill the gerbil, and discretely give the cage back to him. Of course he said he wouldn't come with me, and I did not even want to ask my mother as I knew the answer anyway. I was sick with worry and cried all night. I was firstly upset that the gerbil had died, and secondly I would get the blame for it from Mr Pyle – who I didn't get along with at the best of times. I even thought of missing school on the Monday, but I had nowhere to go. I could hardly walk around Hessle with a gerbil cage in my hand and then donate it to War on Want, without arousing suspicion.

Monday morning arrived and I knew that the other children would think I had killed the gerbil, which I obviously hadn't and I was still distraught. I walked slowly to the school and carried the empty cage into the playground and waited by the school doors. Donna was there, she was a bit mouthy and in my class, she asked where the gerbil was. Luckily just then Mr Pyle was at the door and opened it. Donna told him that I had lost the gerbil, I explained that it had died overnight and was sorry. Luckily Mr Pyle took the cage from me, and told me not to worry and said that the gerbil was old anyway and on borrowed time. At least I had something to write in my diary about the weekend 'the school gerbil died at my house'!

Mother managed to get a job as a school cleaner at Hessle C of E Junior School, the same school as I went to. She only got the job as her Uncle Bernard was the school caretaker and made sure she got it. She would work from 4pm to 6pm, which was fine with us as we could watch television when we got home and play with Dinky. We had at least two hours of freedom without being hit. Sometimes we would just lay on the settee and watch the television and enjoy the peace and quiet. We always had to sit up properly in a regimented position on the settee when my mother was home, so we liked sprawling out best when she wasn't there.

My father cruelly used to turn the television off if he was home early from work, before Mother came back, when we were being quiet watching cartoons. He used to say 'You will get square eyes watching too much television.' I used to say to him that the television isn't even square! Also if we watched Dinky the dog for too long, would we get 'dog shaped' eyes then, and if I read too many books will I get square eyes also? I was always told off for being cheeky or rude, but I wasn't being rude, they were sensible, logical comments. These old wives' tales he spouted were just baloney so he could have an excuse to turn off the television and save electricity. I knew his tricks also. My father was always muttering rubbish quotes and sayings. If Matthew was in bed having a lie in, he would say 'Get up, the sun's scorching your eyeballs out.' Matthew used to retort, 'Well if that's the case I aren't getting up to go outside.' He also got told off for being rude.

I was getting older and fed up of all the stupid sayings Grandma, Mother and Father used to say to us. It was bad enough with the ridiculous nursery rhymes we used to have to read and recite when we were younger, stupid things about a woman who lived in a shoe, and Goosey Goosey Gander and more rubbish, without my father and every other adult quoting such waffle. It was wearing thin on my nerves with the stupidity and nonsensical logic of it all, and then making Matthew learn it – what the hell must he be thinking about it all? The teachers at school would never say such waffle, they seemed quite sensible. There was now a dividing line of who I would believe and respect, and those people were my teachers, not my parents or family.

There was embarrassment when the school sent a letter to Mother to tell her that Matthew had to go to special speech therapy lessons. Mother wasn't happy and I overheard her saying one night to my father that it was because Matthew was a bit 'slow'. She just couldn't grasp the fact that he wasn't allowed to talk at home, and that was why he couldn't speak properly. He could understand everything but becoming mute as he was getting older, and it was now noticeable during his school years with his infant school teacher. I desperately wanted to tell the school that he hadn't a speech impediment or problem, it was because we hadn't been encouraged to speak at home or have an opinion. But who would listen to me? No one. If I told them, then I know my mother would turn it onto me for being a 'liar' or saying I 'exaggerated' things. I noticed that she usually used those words a lot when speaking to teachers or doctors to get herself out of a situation, and then I would get the blame yet again. Let Matthew have his speech therapy lessons, at least it might help him express himself in the lessons, but then he'd have to become introverted when he got home. So really there was no long-term benefit in these lessons. Why could I see that, but no one else could? I daren't even mention my grandma almost brainwashing or scaring Matthew into keeping quiet by mentioning the story of Anne Frank every flaming few minutes at her house. Ramming it down his throat that if he wasn't quiet that the Germans would kill him. He was becoming mentally distressed also. But I noticed my mother had more sympathy for him than for me, he was still gradually becoming her favourite.

This was the year when I really wanted to excel in music at school but was brought down to earth by my mother. I used to play the recorder at school still, but was totally bored with it and wanted to expand my reading of music and play another instrument. This ability was even more heightened when in the April of 1974, ABBA won the Eurovision song contest with Waterloo. To be honest, I wasn't really keen on the song as it was a bit repetitive; it was more the background instruments that I found fascinating. I begged my mother to let me try and play another instrument, even a guitar. But to no avail, she said she couldn't afford it. I was bloody stupid for even asking her, and I hated myself for being so ridiculous and thinking she would actually support me with music. I was now really bored and resentful at home.

I was ten years and my father kept trying to give up smoking, this had been happening for many years so it was nothing new, and he still hadn't given up. He used to try all sorts of methods, such as sucking Polo mints and chewing gum to see if that would distract him. But the chewing gum only seemed to stick on his false teeth or pull them out of his mouth. 'Wrigley's Spearmint Chewing Gum' was the trend at that time, with adverts on television promoting it. I quite liked chewing it also as it seemed to take some of my hunger away. My father didn't approve though, even though he chewed it himself. I used to sneak a gum wrapper out of his cupboard. 'That looks disgusting. You look like you are chewing the cud,' he used to say. When I asked him what this meant he waffled something about looking like a cow chewing grass. I ignored him. However, I had an idea that I would try and chew a whole pack of gum at once, and then see how long it would stretch. But I wasn't sure where to stretch it to measure it. Matthew was messing about in the house so I had an idea. I would chew the gum, then when it was warm and stretchy I would gradually stretch it out of my mouth, on my finger and stretch it like a thin ribbon, and wrap it around his neck. He deserved punishment anyway as he was the 'favourite' child of the house. I kept wrapping thin layers of the gum around his neck, it was really sticking to his skin well and he just stood there and let me do it. It was quite difficult to do it on the back of his neck but I managed. It almost looked like tribal neck rings around his neck, that I had read about once at school.

My father came into the room and went ballistic. He asked what I was doing. I said I was bored. I secretly knew I had gone too far. Poor Matthew had to be dragged to the bathroom sink upstairs for the gum to be washed off with the week old, used flannel and soap. Apparently this was difficult to remove, and he returned ages later with a red raw and still sticky neck. I was secretly laughing to myself about his pain and at times enjoyed getting my revenge on him.

Christmas came and went again this year with the 'Christmas rules' my mother made up becoming more ridiculous year by year. God I hoped I could leave home soon or just stay in bed in my own room on Christmas Day. Matthew and I were becoming more mentally unstable day by day, and Christmas was two weeks of hell. There was a load of trashy programmes on television including musicals and children's films that we were forced to watch. I didn't want to be sociable any longer and wanted to go upstairs and do some of my patchwork quilt in peace and quiet. Obviously I wasn't allowed to. Matthew and I were both so bored we used to make up our own words to Christmas carols and pretend to sing along if they came on television. My father even watched Songs of Praise on Christmas morning. I think he did it to annoy us all to be honest. Our favourite song was 'We Wish You a Merry Christmas'. We changed the words to 'We hope you die at Christmas' – meaning my mother or anyone else that we hated. For God's sake, that is not normal, but still no one seemed to bother about us singing it. We definitely needed some mental help or some medical intervention. I needed to get away. I reluctantly asked my mother if I could go and visit Julie to see what she had got for Christmas, but was told by her abruptly 'No, they don't want you round there on Christmas Day!' I reckon Julie wouldn't have minded to be honest, plus her house was warmer than ours and they had nice food and an open fire.

Christmas was a long, long day for us with the television being switched on and off to suit Mother and Father. They used to make us watch films such as 'The Railway Children' as it was filmed in Haworth, like that was some kind of accolade?! We lived about eighty miles from there, not just around the corner. Just because my father liked trains, we had to endure this boredom. Just as bad was 'Chitty Chitty Bang

Bang', which Matthew and I renamed to 'Shitty Shitty Bang Bang'. Both films were full of spoilt children pretending to act and speak posh. I could not cope with that pretence, it just wasn't realistic and I was a realist. My mother would look through the TV Times or the Hull Daily Mail Christmas TV supplement to see if 'Seven Brides for Seven Brothers' was also on the television. For God's sake, let me just die peacefully now! I hated bloody musicals and still do. All that prancing about and dancing never mind the bad singing – just get to the bloody story line! I was now having that 'glazed look' in my eyes already and Christmas Day wasn't even over with yet.

We were only allowed to open a few presents on Christmas morning, the ones that 'Father Christmas' had left. There were always tangerines, nuts and other fruit shoved in our sacks. Well we both did not like fruit, so it went straight back in the fruit bowl in the room. So that was a waste of time and effort.

Sometimes we got games we could play with, and Matthew would get some Lego bricks. I never got a guitar or musical instrument, as I knew I wouldn't, and was still bitter and upset about it. Other children were outside on their new bikes, whilst we were in a freezing house playing with Lego bricks and my felt sewing set. It was enough to drive us to suicide. The rest of the presents, and presents from our aunties and uncles, were under the Christmas tree. But we could not open them until after Christmas dinner about 3pm or after the Queen's speech.

By this time we'd both given up the will to live as Mother was huffing, puffing and tutting to herself and my father in kitchen. Matthew and I weren't even bothered about Christmas dinner as, if it was anything like a normal dinner time, there would still be arguments. We both did not like

Christmas pudding with its horrible fruit and candied peel in it, and as for the great sherry trifle that Mother would spend hours making, well we hated trifle as well – it tasted like bland custard with a strong hint of alcohol. We would have preferred a custard slice or big cream puff from Skeltons bakery, they were lovely. We usually went without. It was the same with mince pies, we hated those also. But there was always a big drama with Mother baking them herself using mincemeat from a jar and making her own pastry. I used to think, why bother, as there is only herself and my father that liked them? Just go to Grandways and buy some from the bloody shop! We rarely had visitors – in fact I could not remember the last time anyone had even been to the house, so there was no one else to bake for. It was always a big Christmas baking drama. You could almost call it 'The Great Hessle Bake-off'.

No wonder my grandma had changed her religion from Christian to becoming a Jehovah's Witness, I could actually see the attraction of it now. Less stress and no worry at Christmas time! Certainly no baking and buying presents. It was just a normal day in their world. When I visited my grandma I used to read her magazines such as Watchtower and Awake! They were quite 'open' magazines and I would never get this information from my mother's old-fashioned magazines such as Woman's Weekly that were full of knitting patterns, crochet templates and boring sponge cake recipes. In the Jehovah's Witness magazines I could read about all sorts of real-life facts such as abortion, surrogacy and IVF. The things that did puzzle me were the drawn pictures of naked people snuggling up to wild lions and tigers, but my grandma told me it was when they went to heaven or paradise, that was what it was like. But according to her I wouldn't go to heaven as I wasn't a Jehovah's Witness so I would go to hell. This didn't even frighten me, as it seemed like I was in hell most days being at home anyway. It surely couldn't get any worse? My mother had previously told me that she 'hoped I'd rot in hell', so let them both have their own way and beliefs, I was past caring.

Christmas seemed to be for other people to enjoy, certainly not my family. When Top of the Pops came on the television just before the Queen's speech, then the sarcasm started. 'That's not music!' my father would state loudly, as Matthew and I would sing along, this time with the proper words, to groups such as Slade and MUD. 'Turn the television off, Christmas dinner is ready,' my father would then say. That's very convenient, I would think, something that Matthew and I liked and could sing along to, and we had to suddenly turn it off after about ten minutes of watching it. Obviously when we had had our meal, then the television would go back on – just in time for the Queens speech! Very convenient indeed ...

By the time we had opened presents, and then told to write down who we got the other presents from e.g. which aunty and uncle, or neighbour, and what they bought us, we didn't really get a chance to play with any of the presents or games, as it was nearly time for us to go to bed! After watching the boredom of the Queen's speech I would have gladly gone to bed there and then. So much for a happy family Christmas.

CHAPTER 12

Believe and Achieve

All my music lessons and recorder practice with Mr Chignell paid off. Melanie, Jackie, Katrina and myself were excellent at playing the song 'Puff the Magic Dragon' on the recorder, it was one of our favourites at that age. The words didn't really make sense but we didn't care. We also played another one of our favourites 'I'd like to teach the world to sing – in perfect harmony'. We just played and practiced, courtesy of Mr Chignell giving us plenty of music sheets to practice with, and of course his continued patience and guidance. We all loved our recorder practice sessions.

All the practice came to fruition as at the end of the school term in July I was presented with the junior school silver cup for the best pupil in the school for music in 1975, although the other girls did deserve an award also, as we played music together and encouraged each other. When my name was announced during school assembly I could not believe it and was shaking with excitement. My name had already been engraved on the small silver plate on the base of the silver cup along with the year. I was stunned and held onto it until it was time to go home at end of the day. I remember when my father came home from work and saw it, he was trying to polish it with spit and his handkerchief, and placed it on the shelf next to my obstacle race certificate. I cannot remember much encouragement or praise from my mother. I was beginning to realise she was actually jealous of me and hated me even more.

My gymnastic sessions with Mr Bury were also brilliant. I found out that a girl in our class, Debbie, had joined Haltemprice Sports Centre in Anlaby, only a few miles away, for group and individual tuition on gymnastics. She was naturally good at gymnastics and said the club was brilliant and she had learned so much, plus they wore a navy blue and white leotard. The leotard was enough to impress me! She looked the part of a gymnast anyway, as she had long brown hair tied back in a high ponytail, and she had that air of confidence about her that you could tell just in her walk and mannerisms. Debbie said she got the bus from Hessle Square on a Saturday morning to Anlaby, and it stopped right outside the sports centre. She asked if I wanted to come along with her and others that also got on the same bus in Hessle, to tag along, watch what they do, and have a word with the instructor at the end of the session to see about maybe joining in the future. With this excitement in mind and the thought of having some proper tuition, when I got home from school one afternoon I reluctantly asked my mother if I could join the gym club. Obviously the answer was no, with excuses that it was too expensive, she couldn't afford a leotard, bus fares etc. I said I would pay for it myself from my Christmas and birthday money as I was desperate to join. The answer was still no. Oh well, I would resign myself to my bedroom again, and do a bit of work on my patchwork quilt, if I could be bothered. It was as if Mother didn't want me to make friends, go out, or have any hobbies. Looking at the four horrible woodchip painted walls in the bedroom seemed to be the only option I was allowed.

I did look forward to the gymnastics lessons at school where I achieved the B.A.G.A. Gymnastic Awards where you got a certificate and cloth sew-on badge to put on your shorts or leotard. I remember achieving Level 4 at junior school and then moving onto the other levels. I wasn't even sure of the criteria you had to reach to pass these awards. I was just told by Mr Bury to do a handstand, do a cartwheel, do a headstand etc, so just obliged. He must have had a tick-sheet to use as an assessment, as I seemed to pass different levels fairly quickly, as did the other girls. We encouraged each other and compared the coloured badges we received. We sewed them ourselves onto our gym shorts and were all proud of them.

All seemed okay at school at that moment. I had friends and I had achieved so much. At that time school seemed to be fantastic and most of the time was spent doing educational hobbies that I loved: music, sewing, sport, swimming in the school outdoor pool, playing netball, playing rounders. Every day was so enjoyable there and I did not want it to end. Of course we had to do the usual written work such as English, history, geography and maths, but I could cope with these if I had my sport and music.

I was surprised I did so well at school and knew I could do even better if I wasn't so mentally affected by my home life. I had to be a good actress at school and put the bad experiences at home to the back of my mind whilst I was at school, and try to act normal. Whatever 'normal' was. I dreaded going home from school and was always looking at the clock in the classroom, counting down the minutes, but at least Mother now worked until 6pm so I had a bit of respite.

The previous months at home, however, had been horrendous and traumatic. We seemed to have peace and quiet for a week or so at home, but I knew it was too good to last. One afternoon I came home from junior school, unusually Mother was still there and not at work. Matthew was crying and distraught. I thought he might have been naughty and been hit by mother with the Flatley dryer sticks. But through the tears and sobbing he told me that Dinky had been sold. He said that a man had arrived in a small white van, came into the house and collected Dinky, put him on the back seat of his van and drove off. Matthew was upset as he said that Dinky was jumping up and down at the van back windows trying to get out. I ran up to my bedroom as I could not believe my mother could stoop so low and not to tell me that our Dinky was leaving. All night Matthew and I cried. We didn't want any tea, we just wanted Dinky back. We had taught him little tricks such as how to sit and beg for food at tea time and a few other things he loved to do. He was our distraction in the house, and our friend, and SHE had sold him or given him away.

By the time my father came home from work at about 8pm, Matthew and I ran like crazy from our bedrooms and down the stairs to tell him the news. I am not sure if he already knew, but I could tell by his face that he was not happy with Mother. He didn't even question Mother's motives; he could see how upset we were. He was still weak-willed and wouldn't stand up to her. There was nothing I could do. I had to accept that Dinky had gone, I didn't know where, and we would miss him like mad. My mother's cruelty was beyond belief. Why get a dog in the first place, then keep it as a family pet for a couple of years, letting Matthew and myself love it, then just get rid of it? I know the dog always barked when someone came to the door, and also used to chew the mail, but that was dogs for you. He was a terrier after all. Mother seemed to enjoy seeing us all upset. It made her feel important and domineering. I made sure she didn't see me sad, and cried only in my bedroom or the bathroom. I wasn't sure how much more cruelty and hurt she was capable of as there seemed to be no boundaries to her malicious streak. It made me wonder about the school gerbil. What did really happen to him? Did she kill him, or let it escape? I would never know.

CHAPTER 13

Deranged and Estranged

Strangely, that Saturday my father suddenly announced that we were going to go out in the car for a picnic the next day, Sunday. This was highly unusual as the car we had now, another Morris Minor, that was nicknamed Dougal (as in the dog in the Magic Roundabout) didn't go very fast or very far, so it wouldn't have made any great distance. The car even had a massive Dougal sticker on the boot of it, not that that made it go any faster! If travelling up hills, the car would almost be rolling backwards. My mother was saying she wanted to go onto the North Yorkshire Moors, so my father had to oblige. I am not sure whether the outing was a distraction from her getting rid of Dinky. She may have felt guilty, but probably not. We were told to get up early and by about 11am we had to be leaving. Mother was doing a massive picnic for us all and set about making this from about 9am, flasks of coffee for her and my father, and sandwiches for us all. I was not sure of the occasion, if there even was one, or why this was happening, but Matthew and I followed the rules as we were told. 'Her house, her rules', as she kept telling us. It was surreal; I do not think we had ever been on a picnic before. I had lied about going on picnics on my school diary when I was in Mr Pyle's class, but now we were actually going on a real one!

At home we had a garage that was accessible via a tenfoot at the back of the terrace houses on our row. My father had already got the car out of the garage and parked it in the tenfoot. Mother was putting the picnic in the boot of the car, whilst Matthew and I were bouncing on the backseats in anticipation. My father started up the car engine and said to my mother 'Put your seatbelt on then.' She looked at him like he was crazy, then said 'Why?' He began waffling on about safety in the car if they had a car crash and some other boring facts. Bearing in mind that seatbelts were fitted on the front seats of cars in the 1970s but not compulsory to wear. I could see my father's point of view; they were there, so why not use them?

Well something simple, sensible and practical like a seatbelt started Mother off in a tantrum, she snapped and then was shouting, 'If I have to wear one then I aren't going.' My father said, 'Well we won't go then, none of us will go!' Matthew and I were on the backseat of the car cowering. My father actually answered my mother back and we could not believe it, we also couldn't get out of the car as it was only a two door car. We had to endure the shouting, screaming and drama of Mother until she got out of the car in a massive mood, crying, slammed the passenger car door shut and then stormed up the back-garden path to the house. My father told us to stay in the car until she had calmed down and he would stay with us. We waited for what seemed like ages and then all three of us walked with trepidation, my father leading, up the garden path and to the back door that was left wide open. My father went in first and then looked around the kitchen and back room for mother. She wasn't there. He ran upstairs – she wasn't there either. He was shouting her name continually. There was no answer. He guessed she had probably either gone to her mother's house, or got on a bus from Hessle Square to somewhere else – not that there were many, if any, buses, especially on a Sunday from Hessle! She used to threaten she would just go on a bus and never return.

Who knew what thoughts went on in her head? She was seriously deranged.

Father told us to stay in the house and he would get in the car again, drive around Hessle, and see if she was at Grandma's house. We did as we were told as he was clearly upset and so was Matthew. We were both starving as we hadn't eaten in the morning as we were waiting for the great family picnic. My father was in the car, and so was the food, so we still had nothing to eat. I think Matthew was too distressed to eat anyway, but I could eat through all the dramas and it didn't affect me, I had grown used to it by now. We just sat and waited on the settee for my father to return, and bring back mother, I dreaded to think what mood she would be in when she returned. It seemed like we were responsible for her drama and actions and were now being punished. That feeling of uncertainty and dread has never left me to this day. You know, that stomach churning, sick feeling, 'wanting to go to the toilet suddenly' feeling. I hated it then and hate it even now.

After a long time, possibly hours, my father eventually came back home alone. He had spoken to Mother and she was at Grandma's house in Hessle, but she refused to come back home. My father said I now had to be the 'woman of the house' and look after Matthew – little did he know that I did that anyway as best I could. I can't remember if we even ate the picnic or my father had forgotten about it and left it in the back of the car in the sweltering heat of summer. I was hungry, but kept quiet.

The next day was Monday, my father got up for work at the usual time and left us to get ready for school. I was bloody starving. Luckily we still had daily milk deliveries from the milkman so could eat some cereal until that ran out. I gave Matthew some cereal. It was always cornflakes, but the cheap variety, that didn't taste very appetising, but it was something to eat.

My mother used to use the Be-Ro recipe book regularly every Sunday to bake cakes and scones etc. Obviously, she didn't do any baking that Sunday, but there was still some evaporated milk chocolate cake that she had baked and put in a cake tin from the previous Sunday, or even the Sunday before that. I stuffed a load of it in my mouth as I was still starving, but felt sick instantly as it was stale and now had hardened butter cream icing as a filling. I ran outside and was promptly sick in the back garden, but still managed to walk to school with Matthew as if nothing had happened. I was hoping that Mr Bury wouldn't want me to attend his gymnastic sessions at lunchtime as I really didn't feel up to it. I didn't have any money for school dinners so told Mrs Sellers, my current teacher, that I was going home for dinner. Not that there was anything at home to eat and I certainly wasn't going to eat that cake again. I can't remember if Matthew came home at dinner time, but I remember giving him a glass of milk at teatime. I don't think we even locked the house doors as we didn't have a key anyway, but those were the days when you could leave your doors unlocked and no one would bother to try and break in.

Monday was also washing day in most households in those days, but I had seen Mother also wash on a Sunday, so knew what to do, sort of. We had a twin tub washing machine that wasn't exactly easy to use and I certainly couldn't pull it out from underneath the kitchen work surface to sort out and connect all the water hoses etc. I hadn't a clue about the temperature and where the long wooden tongs were that Mother used to lift the wet washing and place it into the spinner. It was just too heavy and too much for me to handle, even at eleven years old. I decided that if I had to do washing

I would do it next weekend in the kitchen sink with water and Fairy washing up liquid. Until then, we would just wear the same clothes. Other families had an automatic washing machine and it seemed really easy to use, but Mother had refused to buy one, I am sure she enjoyed the burden of a twin tub as she was a martyr with all the huffing and puffing and endless comments having to wash using this antiquated method. She used to get a sweat on, and the kitchen was like a bloody sauna from the boiling hot water splashing over the sides of the twintub and onto the floor. Another drama I was also used to. I certainly wasn't going to put myself through such a trauma.

Finding decent food to eat was hard. I managed to find some dry Rich Tea biscuits in a beige rusty biscuit tin and some cooking chocolate drops. At least I could reach the cupboard now without me pulling it off the wall, as I was taller! There were some dry Ryvitas that tasted like cardboard until you put loads of butter on them, and other dry cream crackers. I even buttered Rich Tea biscuits to make them more palatable. In those days there were no convenience foods or microwaves, so you had to make meals from scratch. Not that I even wanted to use the gas cooker or hob, as it frightened me with it being a naked flame. What if I set the house on fire like Mother did all those years ago? How would we get out of the house? All my insecurities and feelings of panic I had locked away in my head from years ago, were now coming to the surface again and I hated it.

One positive that I had forgotten, was every Tuesday the Alpine lorry came down our street and the Alpine man would do lemonade bottle deliveries, collecting the empty glass bottles and wanting payment for the new deliveries. My mother always used to get two bottles a week, usually pink strawberry (soda) lemonade or similar, and dandelion and burdock. These were large glass refundable bottles and the drinks were full of sugar and additives, but in those days who cared? To us children it all tasted fantastic. I came home to find two bottles on the doorstep (and probably a handwritten invoice with what we owed!). Fabulous, at least we had something to drink. Dandelion and Burdock is a bit of an acquired taste, but when you are desperate you will drink anything. I let Matthew have the pink strawberry lemonade as he liked that best. The only other drink we had in the kitchen cupboard was PLJ Lemon Juice that tasted bitter. Mother would drink it when she was on her diet. I hated it.

After we had tried to find something to eat and drink we would sit or lay across the settee, Matthew on one side and me at the other, with coats over us for warmth. I daren't put the gas fire on as mother and father always seemed to struggle to light it, and when it did eventually ignite, it blasted out a massive flame until it settled down. There was no way I was going to try and light the gas fire in case we both got burned or I couldn't turn the gas off. It wasn't too cold as it was summertime, but the house seemed to get cold quickly as soon as the sun went down. We did manage to put the television on to try and distract us. But both cried together as we missed Dinky the dog as he used to keep us warm by snuggling up to us.

My father came back home from work at his usual time, 7.30pm to 8pm. He asked why we were still awake and not in bed, stated that he had eaten and had cooked meals for lunch and tea from the post office canteen, so didn't need anything cooking. Just as well, I thought, as I certainly wasn't putting the oven on, and there wasn't really anything to cook. He didn't have a thought about asking us if we had eaten anything, or if we needed any money for shopping. We both went up to bed hungry and confused and left him downstairs watching the television. My father looked pale, weak and upset, but so were we, and at least he had eaten some hot meals, more than we had.

This routine was to continue for the next few days and became tiresome as we became hungrier but more independent and almost feral-like. I tried to keep the fact that Mother had walked out on us to myself, but just had to mention it to Melanie at school. She confessed that her father had left her mother and family a few years ago. She seemed fairly level headed about her father leaving, so I decided to be like this also, even though it was still raw as it was happening now. Melanie's mother seemed to cope okay, and she had three children to bring up, plus she also attended school plays and sports days, which was more than mine ever did. It got me thinking a lot about family life and how people cope in different situations. I began to realise why Melanie was a bit needier than myself, maybe she felt insecure with losing her father. I didn't ask why he had left – it was none of my business – but I understood her more. I also suddenly felt needy and unwanted.

I was desperately worried about looking after Matthew and how to get hold of food. I thought he might die, and then I would get the blame, and I might go to prison. All sorts of thoughts were going through my head. I didn't know why my mother didn't come home to see if we were okay? Or why didn't my grandma come and see us to make sure everything was fine? We were only a mile away. She was also a coward and this situation proved how much she disliked us also. After all we were just two children aged eleven and seven, forgotten about and left to get on with it, anything could have happened to us. As long as we both still kept going to school and pretending everything was fine, then no one would ever know.

I knew I could trust Melanie not to say anything, but even she didn't know the full story of having no food. I was so jealous of her house and that big farmhouse table with the food in the middle – it was like something you would see in a film or television programme about how the 'other half' live, how I wished we lived there. Melanie certainly wasn't a snob or spoilt, she was the total opposite, but I knew her family had more money than us, and although I did not resent it, I also felt slightly jealous. I even thought about walking to her house, with Matthew in tow, and asking her mother for some leftover food – that is how desperate I was feeling. But I could not bring myself to do it in case we were rejected. I am sure Melanie's mother would have welcomed us and helped us, but I suddenly felt intimidated and out of my depth by her and her house, and it was a big thing to ask for food.

Eventually, after nearly a week, Mother came back home. I think it must have been at the weekend as my father went to collect her in the car, and he worked during the week so wouldn't have taken any time off work, even in these exceptional circumstances! He seemed to think that the post office would stop functioning without him. So we had been left for six days to fend for ourselves. Matthew and I were warned by my father not to speak to Mother as she was still upset. I remember Matthew running up to her when she came through the door. I can't remember her hugging him or saying sorry and that she missed us, as the reality was that she didn't miss us at all, she wanted her freedom. We tried to keep out of her way as we knew she would go ballistic anyway when she saw the state of the kitchen cupboards that were near empty with biscuit wrappers and Ryvita crumbs everywhere, then the empty glass lemonade and milk bottles stacked up on the kitchen sink. I had tried to tidy up the best I could, but now felt depressed and worn out from it all.

Living there now was like 'treading on egg shells' even more, and I hated that and the uncertainty that came with it. I used to stay in my bedroom for the full days on a Saturday and Sunday after that. Mother called me lazy, which I wasn't; I just didn't want to get involved with anything anymore. I distanced myself from my mother and father and hardly told them anything now, in fact I hardly spoke at home, it was better that way. Just like we had been told all those years ago 'children should be seen and not heard', well she had her wish. I didn't want to be seen OR heard, especially at home, as she seemed to think I instigated her outbursts. No wonder our schools thought we were special needs children. Matthew refusing to speak, and me having that 'eyes glazed over, far away look' – I bet they thought we were a right pair of social misfits. Even to this day if I am bored I get the 'glazed-over look'. It must, unfortunately, now be part of my character and one thing I cannot change. All my enthusiasm for school, for life and my hobbies had now gone, almost knocked out of me by Mother. Adults used to look at my sad face and say to me in a jokey way 'Cheer up, it may never happen!' I used to say in a deflated tone 'it already has', and it was the truth, I had nothing to feel happy about. But no one thought to question my answer, and thought I was joking. No one actually asked me 'Why, what HAS happened? Can I help?' No one really cared, it was all lip-service and Matthew also realised this. We were trapped.

CHAPTER 14

Suspicious and Malicious

A few weeks later things seemed to have calmed down. For some unknown reason, Mother decided to get another dog. My grandma had previously rescued a Yorkshire terrier from a local dog's home or somewhere nearby. Her new dog was called Candy and I remember seeing her at my grandma's house and poor Candy had cuts on her face and looked really ill and scared. Grandma said that Candy hadn't been looked after well previously, so she had rescued her. After quite a few months when Candy was better and strong enough, my grandma decided to breed her. She had a litter of puppies and we had one of them. We weren't asked to choose a name, Mother had already named the puppy 'Cheeky'. She said it was a temporary name, but it wasn't. That stupid name stuck with the poor dog until he died many years later.

Cheeky wasn't the same as Dinky, as Dinky was chunky and knew what he wanted; Cheeky was just a small, almost waif-like Yorkshire terrier, but we all loved him just the same. Things seemed to be getting 'on track' again now.

Sometimes Mother was kind to us and would let us have a comic each delivered to the house, along with her Woman's Weekly and my father's monthly copy of Railway Modeller. These were delivered from our favourite newsagents Killingbeck's, which Tony Killingbeck owned and also worked at. I remember he was a lovely man and had time for everyone. Matthew liked the Dandy comic best and I liked the Beano with Dennis the Menace and Gnasher. To be honest it was a bit childish for me now as I was eleven years old, but I still made out that I liked it so Matthew could read it also. I remember us both wanting to join the Dennis the Menace fan club to get a Gnasher badge with fur and wobbly eyes, and my father getting a postal order from the post office to send the form off with a postage stamp for us both. In the post by return we both got a little plastic wallet with a Dennis the Menace badge and also the furry Gnasher one. We both thought it was fantastic, and it did actually make us both happy for once.

We should have known it was too good to last. Matthew's Dandy comic had a free Korky the Cat cardboard glow mask inside it one week. Matthew and I waited until night time, then held the mask up to his bedroom light for a few minutes. I stood on his bed to do this as I was taller, then when Matthew turned the light off, the illuminous paint on Korky's large face, and around his eyes, glowed a yellowy/green colour in the dark and looked quite spooky. We did this a few times the first night and were laughing about it all the time. The next night we tried again. Unfortunately when Matthew turned the light off this time, I must have stumbled or slipped off his bed and caused a loud bang on the floor. Mother was like a released Rottweiler and came almost running up the stairs, as best she could – she was still overweight and unfit.

She found me in Matthew's bedroom and asked what I was doing in there. I said I was looking at the Korky mask and we were making it glow in the dark. She went mad for some unknown reason, telling me I had my own bedroom to go into and shouldn't go into Matthew's, and just ranting at me for no apparent purpose. Any excuse for her to bully and intimidate me. Suddenly, and unexpectedly, she leaned forward and grabbed the Korky mask from Matthew's hand

and ripped it into small pieces! Matthew was screaming, red in the face and sobbing. I was crying because she had just spoilt our fun and we were doing nothing wrong. I also was upset for Matthew as he had really enjoyed playing with the mask. I frantically tried to collect the pieces off the floor and off the bed and was determined to stick them together with sticky tape. I knew I could do it and it would look okay. Mother had now walked out of the bedroom and left us both crying and I had about eight ragged pieces of cardboard in my hands.

I kept the pieces safe under my pillow so Mother wouldn't find them. Especially if she was going to hit me in the bed as she did most nights. I would keep my head on the pillow so they would be safe. The next day I found my father's sticky tape in the sideboard and stuck the mask together. Obviously it did not look brilliant and was lopsided, but I didn't care, she wasn't going to get the better of Matthew and me. I daren't go in Matthew's bedroom again to try it out, so had to give it to him in secret and tell him to leave it under his pillow for safekeeping and see if he could get it to work properly. That was so malicious, how can anyone be so cruel to their children? No doubt Doreen heard the screaming, shouting and crying next door and probably wondered what the hell was going on. By now we knew not to expect anyone to come to save us from that vindictive witch.

I was developing quickly, ready for secondary school and was wanting to gain more information and knowledge. Not that I gained any knowledge from Mother, she didn't seem to know a great deal about anything and could not even start a logical conversation. I couldn't win in that house: if I kept quiet I was then called 'shy' or 'rude' by her and my father, but I didn't really care. If I did speak I got told off or called Moaning Minnie. What the hell was I supposed to do?

I was mentally and physically bored as well as tired out. I wanted to be a gymnast but knew this wasn't feasible, but I would practice to be the best and spent a lot of time down the street doing handstands and cartwheels on the little bit of grass that was in front of the house. I pretended I was taking part in the Olympic Games. I was also surprised Mother didn't tell me off for using that area of grass, as according to her, everything near or in the house was hers. I was sick of reading encyclopaedias as it was all memorising dates and things that were not relevant, or even interesting to me. I wasn't even keen on the boring history books I was forced to buy, and looking back on what allegedly happened many years ago. I just wanted to look forward to the future, which meant leaving school and leaving home. I resented having to save up and spend my birthday and Christmas money on boring books as per Mother's demands. Other children at school got them bought for them by their parents. Melanie had loads of books as I saw them in her bedroom. I had to pay for mine myself at Jennifer Johnson's bookshop in Hessle. I wasn't happy as I wanted to save my money.

I was distancing myself more from the family by staying in my bedroom after having tea, and over weekends. I got bored with sewing the patchwork quilt sometimes, I used to do it when I felt like it, and also got bored of looking at my limited books. I had also a few encyclopaedias which consisted of the Hamlyn Children's Animal World Encyclopaedia and History of the World. I must have read them both numerous times and even they were so boring now. I had to walk to Hessle Library on a Saturday morning if I wanted any other books. But you could not borrow encyclopaedias, they had to stay in the library, much to my annoyance as there were all sorts of things I wanted to learn about. However, I managed to find Enid Blyton's Secret Seven books at the library and loved them, a bit of escapism, and I was addicted to them. Each Saturday I would see if I could go to the library to get the next Secret Seven book. If Mother wouldn't let me, I would tell her I was going to the Remnant Shop to get some more material for my patchwork quilt.

My grandma also had numerous old books. She had a large open cupboard in her spare back bedroom with a load of books on the shelves. They must have cost a lot of money. Some of them I could ignore as they were Jehovah's Witness books and I had no interest in religion. But some of the encyclopaedias were amazing and much better than mine. They were full sets of encyclopaedias, which may have had twelve books in each set, whereas I had only two. There was one set of books about flowers, which sounds boring but it had a fold out area at the back of the encyclopaedia. It had a drawing of a flower that was split into different areas, so you lifted a small overlapping tab and it showed you what was underneath that area of the flower, so for example it broke it down into areas such as petals, stamen, pollen, etc. I would treat these books carefully as I did not want to rip them. I was amazed at how beautiful and colourful they were. My other cousins, however, were not so careful with them and it annoyed me. They didn't really understand. I wished I could take these books home to read in my bedroom in my own time and learn, but I wasn't allowed. I almost begged to my mother to let me borrow them and I would bring them back, but it all fell on deaf ears. I would have to live with my two encyclopaedias and Secret Seven library books then.

My father still worked at the post office but had apparently over the years progressed from jobs such as a telegram boy, postman, working behind the counter at Hessle, driving a TV licence detector van, now to the postcode department. He thought he was important (although no one else did as he was becoming a bit big-headed) as postcodes were fairly new in the United Kingdom. He had been asked to manage this new department at the post office down Lowgate in Hull. He admitted it was a bit of a pain to get from Hessle to central Hull, but he had a car and would get up at some early hour like 6am to get ready and drive to work. This again always woke me up, as he still listened to Radio Humberside blaring out from the battery-operated radio that was on top of the toilet cistern. The headboard of my bed was against the adjoining bathroom wall, so he woke me up early every day he was at work. By the time I had to get ready for school I had already lost 2 hours sleep, but I knew not to complain. 'My house – my rules' as my mother would say, tutting to herself and calling me Moaning Minnie. It was best to just suffer the tiredness and exhaustion of it all.

My father had a collection of postcode directories inside his wardrobe. He didn't have many clothes so used the additional space for his books and paperwork. He had already taught me how postcodes worked, with the different areas of Hull and the different zones and how the numbers progressed from HU1, HU2 areas in the main centre of a city, eventually leading to the outskirts and the small villages. We were in Hessle and our postcode began with HU13. I remember memorising the map of Hull and the other areas and found it quite methodical and easy to understand. My father had other postcode directories for different areas of the UK. It was like an encyclopaedia of postcodes. I would look up loads of addresses e.g. my grandma's, nana's, friends, family who lived in the Hull area. I was learning that a long street had different postcodes for odd and even numbers and may be split in half. I loved it as it was something new to discover. That was until my mother found the directories hidden under my bed (when she was vacuuming) and told me off, then banned me from their bedroom and took them back to father's wardrobe. She should have been grateful that I wanted to learn and read about different subjects. Miserable old cow, I really hated her as she had even stopped me reading. Just because she didn't understand any logic, she had to stop me knowing too much, it was jealousy in case I now got too close to my father. I used to think to myself about how hard my father's job could be. It seemed quite easy to me, learning postcodes, searching postcodes, allocating them to new properties and logging them in one big directory. Bloody hell, I bet I could have done his job twice as quick and more efficiently, and I was still at junior school!

Since I was now banned from reading the postcode directories, I used to sneak the Hull White Pages telephone directory into my bedroom and hope Mother would not notice. The Hull area was, and still is, unique by having its own telephone exchange now run by Kingston Communications. I do remember us having a 'party line' with Doreen next door – this is where two people shared one telephone line (but different numbers) to make it cheaper. Unfortunately, it meant that if one household was on the phone, your 'party line' neighbour couldn't dial out or receive calls at the same time. If you picked up the phone receiver you would even hear their conversation! My mother hardly used the phone as she had no friends to call or speak to anyway.

The Hull phonebook was another revelation to me, I quickly understood the workings of the Hull area phone numbers and the first two digits of the phone number was the area of Hull or surrounding areas. Hessle phone numbers started with the number 64, Anlaby 63 and 21 was Hull city centre, etc. When I was really bored I used to get the phone book out, flick through it, and point to an address at random, and try and work out the beginning of the phone number depending on the area they lived, then I would work out the beginning of that postcode. It was a challenge, almost a quiz, and much better than learning about the history of Kings and Queens of England – forget Jennifer Johnson's expensive book shop that took my birthday and Christmas money. The best things in life were free! However, I felt like I was becoming a recluse and a bore, or maybe just bored. I wasn't likely to go on Mastermind on a Sunday night on the television with my subjects as 'Postcodes and Telephone Numbers in Hull' was I? There must be more to life than this.

I was in the final year of junior school, and was in Mrs Sellers' class, 4S. I really respected Mrs Sellers as I did Mr Chignell the music teacher. Mrs Sellers let Melanie and I sit next to each other in class all the time and seemed to include us in adult conversations more than some of the other children. But she did speak to all the class with respect. She was so knowledgeable; I was in awe of her. Plus she played the piano and we would all sing along – I did not have a good singing voice I must admit, but I would try and sing in tune the best I could! Melanie and I both had our issues, I had more mental and traumatic issues than her, but had to keep things under wraps for the time being. It wasn't a mental cruelty competition. I could easily have told Mrs Sellers about my mother being cruel to us, hitting us, ripping up Matthew's Korky the Cat mask, selling our dog without us knowing, walking out on us numerous times, the list goes on ... but I did not think she would believe me. I could have been wrong. To the outside world I put a brave face on it all, and if the soap opera 'EastEnders' was around then, I would have made a brilliant actress as I was used to acting each day at school as if nothing was wrong. The only personality issue I really had was that I was unintentionally a bit snappy and could be almost rude to people. But my stomach was churned up every day from lack of food and also stress. I think in those circumstances I had a right to be a bit bloody snappy.

I was so physically tired from everything. When Mother was home I would be walloped in bed for no reason when I was in bed trying to sleep, so I daren't sleep at night. When she wasn't there, I had Matthew crying in the night so had to comfort him, get him a drink of water or whatever he wanted, and then get him ready for school. I was literally a tired, knackered, shattered, clumsy, walking disaster. If other children had to walk in my shoes for a day, they would not get far. Take it from me, my shoes were still too small as I was accused of 'growing too quickly', so didn't get any new ones as Mother has apparently spent all my dad's housekeeping money on food and could not afford any shoes. I did not show any emotion in front of Mother. The only emotion I showed was in private, which was to cry in my bedroom about Dinky being sold and sometimes sob if I was cold and hungry, and also if my feet hurt with blisters from my tight shoes hurting me.

I did, however, feel safe and secure with Mrs Sellers and I wished she was my mother. If she WAS my mother I would certainly do anything she wanted, I would wash and dry the pots for her after teatime, tidy up, and also say 'please' and 'thank you'. Unfortunately, this was just a fantasy, even she didn't know the full story of my life. My mother was a good liar and made out to people that I had a vivid imagination or told lies, which could not be further than the truth. Mrs Sellers did treat all her pupils the same, but I felt she did favour Melanie and I, though maybe I was clinging onto some hope that someone actually liked me.

At parents' evening, Mrs Sellers would say how talented I was with my P.E. (sport and gymnastics), music and English, the subjects I loved and used to get good grades for on my school report. She would also tell my mother that I was polite. Mother came back home to tell me this, and said she questioned Mrs Sellers if she was speaking about the correct child, as according to Mother she had told Mrs Sellers that I was never polite and didn't even speak at home! I just agreed with Mother as it was easier to agree than say I wanted Mrs Sellers as my mother instead.

There was a last school trip, a residential one, to the Lake District and everyone was going except me, it was for five days in a youth hostel. Mother said that I would be travel sick, so I couldn't go. I think it was more the case of she would not pay for me to go. It was true that I was travel sick on the double decker bus to Hornsea that took almost two hours to get there, but I wasn't sure about the Lake District. But she had made her decision. Now during lessons we learned about the Lake District, Ambleside and climbing Helvellyn and all the different walks and the geography of the land. I had to listen to the others talking about staying for five days at the Lake District, in a youth hostel and sleeping in dormitories. Even Melanie was going. When the class went on their trip I had to go into another class for that week and just sit at the back of the classroom and listen to lessons. I was truly bored, didn't want to be there and I missed my school friends.

When everyone returned to school the following week, they said they had a fantastic time and told me of all the adventures they got up to. It sounded like the Secret Seven adventures! I was jealous but also pleased for them. It wasn't their fault that I didn't go, it was my mother's. I was the 'odd one out' again with some of the other children in the class asking why I didn't go with them and genuinely confused as to why. I made numerous excuses, and felt I had missed out on so much over those few days.

Near the end of the school term in July, Mrs Sellers announced there was a walk she would like us all to go on. I hated bloody walking but kept quiet. It was a walk from the school via Hessle Foreshore and following the River Humber to somewhere near North Ferriby. It was about six miles and an afternoon's walk of a few hours. I told my mother that I needed to take a drink with me and Mrs Sellers said we were not allowed to wear trainers or plimsolls, and had to use walking shoes or strong shoes. Obviously, all the other children that had gone on the Lake District trip a few weeks prior had proper walking shoes. Unfortunately, I didn't. Mother would not pay for some walking or strong shoes for me as she said she was sick of my feet growing so fast and she could not afford them. My feet were size seven, I admit, but I was tall and in proportion, and it wasn't my fault my feet were growing all the time. Matthew was the same, massive feet for a child, we called them canoes! My only solution was that I had to use some of my old shoes that were at least one size too small for me. I remember putting them on my feet and the only way I could walk was if I clawed my toes downwards like an eagle's. It was uncomfortable to walk even a few steps, but I had no choice.

On the day of the trip to North Ferriby, we all set off walking from the school in Northolme Road, Hessle and onto Hessle Foreshore. Even by that time my feet were already killing me, and I had blisters on the back of my heels and on my toes as they were cramped up in tight shoes. I felt like taking them off but then other children would be laughing at me. I wouldn't mind but some had turned up in plimsolls, and had gotten told off, but at least if I had worn plimsolls I would be able to walk without pain. I remember walking and could feel every step in those shoes. It was agony. The boys in our class had run ahead of us girls and were pointing to something on the mud on the foreshore covered with white pebbles and stones. As we approached it we could see it was a dead dog, which looked like a boxer dog, that had been washed up on the foreshore, probably someone's pet. For God's sake, what a bloody day. The lads were poking at it with sticks and being told off by the teachers. I could not wait to get back home and take off my shoes, my toes were blistered so much I could have cried with the pain. It took about a week for my feet to recover, but no one seemed to care. Instead I got told off by Mother for using all the sticking plasters and tissues from the cupboard at home. The next day at school, we had to write an essay about the walk. I think we were supposed to write about the River Humber and the geography and landscape, all I could think of writing was about my sore, blistered feet from my tight shoes, and the sight of the dead dog!

This was also the year that our class would undertake Cycling Proficiency Training at the school. The only snag was I did not have a bicycle. I now had to spend my remaining birthday money from aunties and uncles on a bike, as I stupidly presumed that I may get one as a present the previous Christmas. No, I was wrong, so as well as encyclopaedias that I had bought, read and thought were boring, I now had to put my spare money towards a new bike. There was a bike shop at the top of my grandma's street called Richardson's. When you went into his small shop it always smelled of oil and leather. Mr Richardson was usually friendly to his customers as I think he was the only bike shop in Hessle, so he would have hiked up his prices to get a good profit. Not that I blamed him, anyone else would do the same. I wanted a bike like a Raleigh Chopper or even a racer bike, the racers looked like you could get a good speed up on them. Oh no, I wasn't allowed one of those, my mother and father said when we were in the shop, I had to buy a nice 'girls or ladies' style bike. I was fuming but restrained myself. I ended up paying some money to Mr Richardson and my father paid the rest for an Elswick Hopper Safeway ladies' bike. It was red with white writing on and looked smart but it wasn't what I wanted. But I didn't have an opinion or a choice. I was determined to get a woman's racer bike when I left school and went out to work and could afford it. I would show Mother her favourite saying 'I want, never gets' was absolutely rubbish. If I want it, I will get it. It made me more determined to prove her wrong – and I did a few years later when I bought a metallic grey and blue ladies racer and absolutely loved it.

I remember taking the Cycling Proficiency Test, and the playground in the junior school being marked out with different lanes and small traffic lights. We all stood in line with our bikes awaiting our turn on the make-believe lanes, and I felt the odd one out as everyone else had a Chopper or another similar bike. I seemed to have an adult's bike that was far too big for me to even ride, and my feet did not even reach the ground properly. We all passed our Cycling Proficiency Test (God knows how!), and were presented with a small triangular metal badge and a certificate at assembly that Friday by Mr Phillips.

At the next school assembly, Mr Phillips announced that it would soon be time for the older pupils (my year group) to move to their secondary school. But before we did this, we would go to visit their next school. We all had to walk from Hessle C of E Junior School, up Northolme Road and along Beverley Road, and across Boothferry Road, to Hessle High Lower School. This was the only secondary school in Hessle. The site was split into two, with the upper school nearly a mile away in distance at the top of Boothferry Road. We all walked with the junior school teachers, and with some trepidation, to the secondary school. We then followed the teachers into the school assembly hall to find out which forms we were allocated for September. Looking around, the hall was massive compared to the junior school one, and also really noisy with chatter. There were what seemed like hundreds of pupils there, but in reality there were probably about 200. There were children I had never seen before, from other schools such as Penshurst, schools in Anlaby and those on Boothferry Estate who were on the outskirts of Hessle and didn't want to go to their first-choice secondary school in Hull.

At the front of the hall Mr Svenson was now on the stage, and with a raised voice introduced himself and told us all to be quiet. He was a plump man with rosy red cheeks, I think he was the deputy head teacher, but I can't honestly remember. One of the children sat behind me said to another, 'Oh he's the one who fell off the stage once, my brother told me.' Everyone started laughing and Mr Svenson told us all to be quiet again in a stern voice. Bloody hell, he would get on well with Mother, I thought to myself. He welcomed us all to the school and gave a speech about the school and some boring historical facts about it. Then he said he would ask individual teachers to call out who was in their forms, and if your name was read out, you had to quietly follow the appropriate teacher to the classroom.

The order of the forms was a bit strange, and they were split into 'A' and 'T' forms, so it ranged from A1, A2, A3 and A4, then T1, T2, T3 and T4. With A1 being the highest level and T4 the lowest. I still haven't a clue what the letters 'A' and 'T' stood for! Students' names were called out and they followed the appropriate teacher to their designated class-room. The names were called out in reverse class order of T4 up to A1. I was still sat there when they were calling out names for the A1 class. I thought I had missed hearing my name being called out with all the noise in the large school hall, but no, my name was suddenly then called out. I was sure they had made a mistake but who could I tell? No one. I just followed the form teacher, Mrs Raymond, to her ground floor classroom with the rest of the class. Mrs Raymond was well-groomed, her blonde hair was set with hairspray and immaculate, her clothes were expensive, brightly coloured and nicely fitted, and she spoke with sophistication. I could tell she was passionate about her role in the school and I held onto her every word. This was a whole new chapter to me.

I was so nervous but also excited, after all, maybe I wasn't as thick, horrible and as naughty as my mother made out, I was sure she would be so pleased for me, to be in one of the top forms in the school. How wrong I was. When I got back home from Hessle High School I told Mother I was in class 1A1. 'What the hell is 1A1?' she almost shouted as if I had done something wrong. *'Just forget it,'* I thought to myself. It wouldn't have mattered to her if I was in the top or the bottom class. I knew I would have to work like crazy to achieve the levels of the highest class. It was okay being near the top of the class in junior school, but now I was with the top of all the other classes from other schools, so had to prove myself and keep on learning. This was hard to do in our house with no parental support or educational books, along with my already high anxiety levels. I would worry about that in September, after I had the usual school summer holidays and the annual family caravan holiday to Hornsea first. I was not looking forward to that either.

CHAPTER 15

Hurtful and Hateful

I remember the week staying at the caravan in Hornsea, it was a boiling hot week at the end of August, starting on the Bank Holiday weekend. The usual week our family were allocated a seven-day holiday in my grandma's caravan each year. All the other family members, and anyone else who asked to stay, bagged the earlier school holiday weeks for July and August. We had the 'end of school holidays' slot at the end of August and beginning of September, when the nights were drawing in and the weather was getting cooler. I think my father liked that week best as he only had to take 4 days holiday off from work, as it was a Bank Holiday Monday, rather than five full working days. That's if he even came with us; most of the time he didn't. Looking back, I never really knew when he took his other holidays from work as he was always at work. Mind you, Hornsea was never a holiday for me I can tell you.

As we got older we realised that there was nothing to do inside or outside of the caravan. We had no radio, unless we brought a portable radio with us (along with numerous spare batteries, those big chunky ones that cost a fortune) and had no TV as we had no electricity in the caravan. I used to bring numerous books with me, mostly acquired from the charity shops in Hessle, or from the library. I did enjoy reading, to be honest. I realised that some of the books were boring but still used them as a 'cover' for sitting in the corner of the caravan and being quiet and keeping out of others' way, as I always seemed to be either in the way or doing something wrong, even when I wasn't! Even when I sat down or breathed, I did it wrong, according to Mother.

To get rid of us during the day Matthew and I were allowed on the beach without supervision. Looking back I think Mother was hoping we would be abducted by someone, or washed away into the sea, so she could have a quiet life. But we always came back at tea time, much to her annoyance, probably. Even the beach was boring and we used to get badly sunburned as we were both fair skinned and there was nowhere to shelter. The most exciting thing we found to do was clambering up and down the cliffs without falling to our death!

Usually the wooden steps leading down to the beach from the caravan site on the clifftop would be washed away by the tide each year, and it took the council (or whoever had the responsibility of the steps) ages to replace them. Instead of walking about half a mile to the next steps or slope down the cliffs, we would just clamber down the cliffs with our flip flops on, or even just sit on a cliff ledge halfway down the cliff, just watching the sea and pretending to look out for whales or dolphins. Obviously at this age, and in 1975, we did not know how much the cliffs were unsafe and crumbling. Coastal erosion wasn't really mentioned in those days.

The options on the holiday for Matthew and I were quite restrictive when you have no money: sit in the caravan and keep getting told off, sit outside the caravan near the smelly ditch with nettles and potty wee in it and Mother still moaning and telling us off, sit on a cliff ledge and watch the sea or finally clamber down the cliffs and walk on the sand getting severe sunburn as we went walking along. I was encouraged to get 'some sun on your back to dry up all your spots' by Mother, when in fact it would just probably give me skin cancer later in life. My face and back were always as red as a lobster as my skin would burn like crazy, become painful by night time and feel like it was on fire. We usually chose the latter, and would walk for what seemed like miles, looking for unusual seashells or fossils either in the cliffs or at the bottom of the cliffs on the sand, trying to keep in the shade. Matthew and I would also sit and watch the jets fly near Hornsea across to the bombing range at Cowden, and also wave for ages to the yellow RAF Sea King helicopter that used to regularly fly across the Hornsea coastline.

I remember thinking that when I went to the caravan with my Aunty Linda (my mother's sister who was ten years younger than her), that she was totally different to my mother, and she gave me loads more freedom without constantly whinging at me. She enjoyed playing bingo, so every night we would all walk along the crumbling clifftops to the local amusement arcades and get some pennies off her to play the penny machines, whilst she played a few games of bingo. I loved playing the penny machines and going to my favourite amusements. Sometimes it baffled me that my aunty wasn't nagging and shouting at me, as my mother's voice and tutting was now a constant echo in my head permanently.

Mother complained about everything she could, from the way I spoke (so I learned not to speak that much and then got accused of being shy and ignorant, or told 'who asked YOU?'), the way I walked, ('get your hands out of your pockets' she used to shout), to the way I ate (I learned to eat fast in case the food was taken away from me when she had one of her temper tantrums). Whatever I did or said it was never good enough for her. I gave up trying to please her and just seemed to exist and jump through her hoops on demand, a bit like an animal in a circus act.

Matthew was just as bad as me (remember he had to go to speech therapy as he didn't speak and they never knew why. Well that's the reason – Mother!), he never got told off as much as myself as, apparently, I should be 'setting a good example to him' as I was the eldest child. But who was setting an example to me? I used to think this to myself. I certainly wouldn't be using my mother's behaviour as a 'good example'. Also why was I suddenly responsible for other people's actions? Matthew was never going to be a quiet, intelligent, obedient brother, yet I now seemed to be blamed for that also.

I was really interested in the sort of fantasy world of the Enid Blyton Secret Seven and Famous Five books. I loved these books but even I knew at an early age that these were not true. The Secret Seven gang would go exploring on a beach and find smugglers' caves, pirates and secret stashes of jewellery in treasure chests. All we had on Hornsea beach was a few broken seashells near the shoreline, smelly seaweed and fossils in the cliffs, nothing like caves and smugglers.

One night, on our annual family holiday, I was sat quietly in the caravan with my books, minding my own business when Mother did the usual sneaky trick of grabbing me and forcing my body down so she could pick and squeeze my spots on my face. For God's sake, there was no respite even on a so-called holiday. 'It's the badness coming out of you!' she kept telling my father and Matthew, almost spitting the words out in excitement, like she was possessed by the devil. This was now getting repetitive and boring and more painful the older I got. The whole bloody caravan site could hear her as the caravan walls were the width of a tin from a tin of baked beans, not insulated, and her high-pitched, screeching voice just travelled, and was probably heard by dogs a mile away. Even in the caravan she could not control herself.

I had learned to be almost self-sufficient and never complained; I just got on with it, I had to. This resulted in me keeping illnesses to myself, e.g. toothache/headache/earache/flu, in fact any ache or pain. I never used to tell her as it showed I had a weakness, plus she would tell anyone that would listen to her such as my grandma or even Doreen, nothing was kept confidential or private, she enjoyed spreading gossip. I wasn't well. I remember before the end of the school term having bleeding, I wasn't sure where from. It happened when I went for a wee – I was not sure if it was from my bladder or other areas. The toilet bowl was full of bright red blood and I had a massive stomach ache. I was so scared of telling anyone – so I didn't. To this day I do not know what was wrong with me. I was frightened and felt physically sick, but I had no one to tell. I just went to school and carried on as normal. The bleeding eventually subsided after a few days, so I forgot about it. 'Out of sight – out of mind', as my mother would say. Unfortunately, I had also felt run down and ill for the past few weeks or so, but also kept this quiet. I preferred to suffer in silence than have her laughing at me. Not knowing how I really felt, which was 'as sick as a dog', Mother continued with the spot-squeezing on my face and in my ears, firstly with her sharp fingernails and then moving onto hairgrips to press the rounded end onto my spots to cause even more pain and scarring!

She was prodding about in my ears, I was crying with pain and trying not to be sick, and then she feels a lump under my right ear, she suddenly stops still – like an animal waiting to pounce on its prey. It was probably an inflamed spot or something, not really that important. I was telling myself this in my head and hoped it didn't feel as big to her as it felt to me. It felt almost egg shaped and heavy. Mother suddenly pounces with her sharp fingernails and tries to squeeze it hard, as if it is a boil and will burst, causing me to shout and cry out in severe pain. My father, who is sitting next to her, tells her to stop it, but she carries on squeezing and then shoves me on the floor of the caravan, as she cannot get it to burst. Obviously by this time I am in a heap on the floor with a painful, swollen ear and crying out loud from the pain. My father tried to reason with her but she's not having any reasoning. She then yells at me, telling me that I'll be dragged to the doctors tomorrow; I try and hold back more tears.

Well that was easier said than done as our doctor was in Hessle, not Hornsea. The next day my father was tasked with the job of taking me to any random doctor and finding out why I had a lump under my ear. I wasn't bothered by this, as at least I would be away from Mother and would be by myself with my father, and fairly safe in the car. I think we tried Hornsea Hospital first, but they couldn't treat me, so we went to the nearest doctor in the town that they recommended.

The doctor's surgery was down the main street in Hornsea town centre, I remember the room was down a long corridor. It was old, dusty and fusty smelling. It was a male doctor who saw me and he confirmed it was my glands that were inflamed, and prescribed antibiotics. My father and I both went to the chemist nearby to get the antibiotics, which turned out to be in capsule form. Unfortunately, we didn't realise this until we got back to the caravan site. That's when the next saga happened.

I was now eleven years old and couldn't swallow tablets at all. I couldn't even swallow small travel sickness tablets and had to crunch them to swallow them, they tasted disgusting. Back at the caravan my father gave me a cup of water to swallow the first antibiotic tablet, I started choking on the tablet that was now stuck in my throat and I began coughing and spitting the water out of my mouth. Mother, who was now in a temper, grabbed me by my clothes, opened the caravan kitchen door and threw me outside the caravan onto the paving slabs below, with a cup still in my hand, to attempt to swallow the tablet outside instead. As if going outside would make any difference?! By this time I was sobbing uncontrollably from the shock of being literally grabbed and unexpectedly thrown down the caravan steps, and could hardly breathe never mind take a tablet. I tried to swallow another tablet but I choked on it and it came out of my mouth in a fountain of water almost like projectile vomiting. I could see the capsule coating, a bright colour on the paving slabs below my feet, I knew I hadn't swallowed it, so I kicked it into the grass between the paving slabs and then crushed it deeper into the grass heavily with my foot. Bollocks to it, I thought, I don't want the tablets anyway.

By this time there was water all over the paving slabs so I was hoping the capsule would dissolve anyway. I should have known different. Matthew came outside at that time, he was probably hiding inside the caravan away from the abuse and shouting. He must have seen me spit the tablet out from inside the caravan and went straight to the area where I had been. He shouts out 'Look the tablet is on the ground!' Bloody big mouth almighty! My father came outside and saw the half mangled up capsule between the slabs, now squashed into the grass. He looks at me and then raises his hand to hit me across my face. He slapped me so hard across my cheek that his watch strap broke and the whole watch literally flew off his wrist and into the ditch at the side of the caravan that was full of six-foot high nettles, weeds and piss from the piss-potty, plus other unthinkable things such as rats and other vermin. He then had to go into the ditch to try and retrieve the watch. So I got the blame for that also! I cannot even remember if he found his watch and I didn't, and still don't, care. I only had to be near my mother or father and I'd get the blame. I tried to keep away from them all but there was no escape in a small caravan.

My mother began screaming and shrieking at me like a fishwife for about half an hour, about me breaking my father's favourite watch. As if it was my fault he had slapped me so hard. He had broke it himself! My father then shoved me into the car and said that we were going back to the chemist where we got the tablets from. Nowadays the police probably would have been called to the caravan site, but like I already knew – no one really cared or would believe me. I had to sit quietly in the car and then go into the chemist with him where he produced the mangled up, soggy and ripped packet of tablets and explained that I could not swallow them and could I have some other medicine instead? The chemist obliged but only, as I suspect, that they saw the state of me with large red, puffy eyes from crying, a runny nose, a massive bright red slap mark across my cheek, crumpled clothes and water splashes all down my top. This was definitely a case for social services, but again, who cared? No one. Nothing was said or even questioned at the chemists. We returned to the caravan and all seemed okay. Even though the medicine tasted horrid, compared to the capsules, it was palatable. I certainly wasn't going to complain.

The next day of the holiday there were more dramas involving water and fire in the caravan, to be honest it was a wonder that bloody caravan was still standing.

Mother had decided to do some hand washing, I don't know why as we were only there about seven days and only lived about twenty miles away. If we needed spare clothes my father could have driven back home. I remember Mother was there, as large as life, carrying a bucket full of soapy water out of the caravan, full of underwear or something similar. Some of the water must have dripped onto the lino on the small kitchen floor, and she slipped and fell backwards, the full bucket of water falling backwards onto her. She was covered from head to toe with soapy water and dirty underwear. There was literally a flood in the kitchen as the floor space was only about two metre square, if that. If there had been CCTV around at that time I could have made some money on social media with that video.

My mother always had her hair cut, permed and styled like the Queen's or Queen Mother's. You know, the old-fashioned poodle perm, the style NEVER to be changed. She went each week to Top Knot, a hairdresser in Hessle, for a shampoo and set, like old people did in those days. Well now her hair looked like the wet poodle look with small poodle curls on short hair. Mother started screaming, blaming us, even though Matthew and I were actually outside the caravan looking in and saw it all. As usual we get the blame again! She was whinging that her clothes were all wet and she'd have to go to a salon in Hornsea for her hair to be shampoo and set again. So my poor father had the duty of taking her to any random hairdressers in Hornsea. Matthew and I just sat outside the caravan waiting. They eventually came back and her hair looked a bit better, well at least it was dry. She was still huffing, puffing and tutting about it though, probably to annoy us. We ignored her and her dramas.

She then decided to cook some dinner, as by this time it was the middle of the afternoon and we had eaten nothing, I suppose in those days food and eating weren't high on the agenda and we used to go without quite often, so any food was a bonus.

The kitchen facilities were quite limited in the caravan, there was a two-ring gas hob with a small oven/ grill. My mother didn't try to use the hobs or oven too much as, if the Calor gas cylinder ran out of gas whilst she was using it, she would have to pay for another one. She didn't want that added expense. So it was a rarity that she cooked in the caravan. However, today, Mother decided to cook some sausages for dinner – the fact that I hated sausages was beside the point, it was either eat the food or starve.

Matthew and I were sat outside on some orange, stripy coloured deckchairs, with the windbreaker up against the caravan for shelter. The next thing we hear is the fat warming up and hissing in the pan, Mother adds the sausages, and then suddenly the frying pan is on fire in the caravan kitchen, some of the lard, or whatever fat was used, must have gotten too hot. The whole bloody pan is on fire and flames wafting up to the low ceiling of the caravan.

God knows how she was going to put it out, it all happened so quickly. All I remember is that as Matthew and I were sat outside, we saw the whole pan being thrown out the caravan door, flames, fat and sausages! If the flames had actually touched the caravan, it would have set the whole lot on fire within a few minutes. Remember this was in the 1970s, the times before suitable fire regulations and decent fire blankets or extinguishers! I don't think we had any dinner that day and no wonder I'm mentally traumatised from the events of that holiday. Other people go on holiday to relax, I needed a holiday to forget about that one! I now felt on the verge of a bloody mental breakdown.

After the so-called Hornsea holiday, it was time to go back to school just a few days later.

My first day at school was nerve-racking. I walked to Hessle High Lower School with Julie and we met a few others along the way, so we all walked together. I had a new leather school satchel that already hurt my right shoulder and by the time I got to school I was feeling lopsided from the weight of it, and that was when it was almost empty! I was wearing a 'mix and match' uniform and felt like a bit of an outsider already.

My school blazer was from War on Want, bought in that shop years before in preparation for my first day at school. It was heavy as the material was like a thick and woollen knit with old-fashioned piping in navy and white, around the pocket and sides. It had the school badge embroidered onto it. It still smelled of moth balls from the charity shop, even though I had sprayed it with cheap Avon perfume of my mother's that I found in the bathroom cabinet. Looking around at the other students, I noticed that they had thinner, lighter modern polyester blazers, with no piping, and also a newer school badge than what I had. My body was flaming boiling hot and sweating already from the thickness of my blazer and the half-hour walk to the school. I was sure it was a boy's blazer from at least forty years previous as the logo and style was so different to what others were wearing. I was the odd one out already. Flaming charity shop, and also Mother being tight with her money and not buying me a new one!

The only new items I was wearing were a navy-blue skirt, a pale blue long-sleeved polyester shirt, navy v-neck jumper and a tie bought from Gordon Clarke, a well-known school uniform shop based under the city hall in Hull. I had to go there with my mother and father for them to choose my uniform, like I was about five years old! Well 'mix and match' did not really work very well at school when you were in the top form and dressed in part old-fashioned clothes from War on Want. I was so embarrassed as no other children seemed to be dressed like me. I even wore girls' white knee-high socks, when others wore navy blue ones. Some of the Penshurst girls in the class had already sniggered and called me 'virgin' because of my white socks. Even the hairs on my legs poked through them as I wasn't allowed to shave my legs, or so Mother had told me. You know that old wives' tale 'if you shave the hairs on your legs, they will grow back thicker and quicker', well Mother believed it. I just wanted to go home, but couldn't as I'd get told off by my mother for going home. She would go berserk if I mentioned the uniform and I would be called 'ungrateful', which she seemed to throw into every sentence she said to me nowadays. I now sat in Mrs Raymond's class, trying to listen to her, but could have cried.

I now hated school, gone was the protection of the junior school and encouragement of the teachers there like Mrs Sellers, Mr Bury and Mr Chignell. There were no role models like my previous teachers and I was out of my comfort zone and it was scary. Now it was just as bad as being at home. I had that sick feeling in my stomach and wanted to go to the toilet. There again, I wasn't even allowed to go to the toilet at school, as a teacher stopped me one break time and said I should have gone at lunch time! To me this was another adult bullying tactic like my mother's traits, making the rules up as they go along. The teachers bullied the students as much as the students bullied each other!

During the next few weeks, I was being bullied by some of the ex-Penshurst school girls, this time not for my white socks but for being good at music, and also as I wanted to learn the clarinet. They would throw my school exercise books out of my locker and onto the floor in the corridor then rip them, then they would hit me on the head. It was six of them onto myself, that wasn't fair. Ironically big Joanne from all those years ago down Gladstone Street was one of those bullies. She would never change. All I told myself was thank God I went to Hessle All Saints School instead of Penshurst. Obviously respect for others was not taught at that school for those certain girls. I would have hated to be a bully like they were; it is a despicable action – they have to live with that, I don't. I told Mrs Raymond about the bullying once and she was really sympathetic and did 'have a word' with those girls, but it made them even worse as they called me a 'grass' – again I was trapped, still bullied, and certainly didn't want to go to school.

On a positive note, I was loaned a clarinet and case from the school and had music tuition once a week with a peripatetic music teacher that the school hired for the students that were gifted in music. It was my sanctuary – no bullying with peace and quiet in one small classroom. I had clarinet lessons with my good friend Melanie (who was now in a different class to myself), so it was almost private sessions together. This was free and we did really well together and learned lots more about reading music. We kept practicing and playing music together in the school and at home. Although Mother used to complain that I was playing the clarinet too loudly in my bedroom, so I used to try and play it inside my wardrobe to muffle the noise. This probably annoyed the neighbours like mad. Music did not always come naturally to me, but I could read music well, memorise it and even enjoyed playing percussion instruments. I loved being in the school orchestra, where we would travel into Hull and to other secondary schools to play in concerts after school. Some of our favourite tunes to play now in the orchestra were 'Eye Level' and also some of 'The Sorcerer's Apprentice' music. The woodwind section was a pleasure to be in, and our friend from junior school, Jackie, played the oboe along with Melanie and myself in the orchestra.

I was now used to my parents not coming along to the concerts and school orchestra competitions the school participated in. Our school orchestra was really good and we won loads of trophies and awards. It was just embarrassing when the music teachers would ask where my parents were. I would say they were at work, or tell some other lie. The most embarrassing thing was that the school minibus would take us from school and into Hull to the city hall, or wherever the venue for the concert was, but then it was expected that your parents would be there to watch you perform and then give you a lift home. Obviously this didn't happen for me, and I had to cadge a lift home from another student's parents back to Hessle.

Usually after the concerts there was a buffet and drinks. Melanie's mother always came to see Melanie play the clarinet and would indulge in a glass of wine (for adults only!) and sandwiches – it made me chuckle to be honest as I could not imagine my mother doing that. She certainly wouldn't have any wine or enjoy herself. Melanie and I would nibble at the sandwiches and small cakes. I didn't want to show how hungry I actually was, as I would have eaten like a feral cat if I could. But I had learned to show some decorum at appropriate times.

It gave me a thrill to be able to do something I enjoyed and wasn't criticised for, and actually be rewarded with praise, although I still had great anxiety issues if the music teacher did pull me up on something to correct me. I had to try not to reply back with sarcasm or be snappy, I had to remember it was not my mother speaking to me (it was a man anyway) but he was giving me some important information about how to play correctly and improve. I had to accept this, and I convinced myself to change my attitude and not take everything personally and critically. Obviously a hard thing for me to do, but I tried so hard.

Then it suddenly all went downhill near the end of the first summer term after I had a full year of music tuition. The school now decided to charge something like 10p a session for music tuition. It had been free before, but the school now had to charge a nominal fee for the hire of the instruments and tuition. I knew that my mother would not pay that amount of money so I had to find other ways of finding money. I used to try and find money in the house to pay for the lessons, e.g. hand down the back of the settee, sneak into my mother and father's bedroom and look in my father's bedroom top drawers, as he always used to put his loose change in the top drawer (I found this out). I even used to look on the pavement and in the grass in the street for money. Just to keep this private tuition going a bit longer. I was devastated when I had to admit to the peripatetic music teacher that I could not afford the music lessons anymore (after all the pavements were not paved with gold, and I couldn't find any more money however hard I looked), and I had to hand back my clarinet. It was a sad, emotional day and I had nothing to look forward to anymore. I had loved the orchestra and the comradeship amongst us all. Also, I did not know what had happened to Melanie as I could not find her in the school playground anymore. Little did I know at the time that her mother had moved house away from Hessle and relocated the whole family. She had moved schools. I would now not see her until some twenty years later when our paths would somewhat ironically cross at work by pure chance.

CHAPTER 16

Progression and Regression

It was 1976, I was twelve years old and I craved to escape to anywhere. I wasn't bothered where, as long as I wasn't in that house anymore with Mother. She had made me mentally, emotionally and physically tired and my body and brain wanted to shut down from being so stressed from the anxiety. I was tired of all the hitting, of not being able to sleep at night due to the nightly pyjama-gate thumping, tired of all the spot-squeezing causing unnecessary pain and tears, I was even tired and worn out from my own sobbing into my pillow every night and then waking up with a violent headache the next morning, along with my red puffy eyes. I had to withhold my emotions otherwise Mother would have won, but I was finding it more and more difficult to do this. I was still an emotional wreck and she would have loved to see me crack under the pressure. It was like she was almost waiting for me to explode or erupt like a volcano, then if I did, it would then allow her to physically hurt me even more. I had to control myself. By now I hated my mother, father and school immensely, I needed an escape from life in general. I actually realised why people committed suicide – to get away from being terrorised daily. I felt I was in a prison and being mentally and physically tortured constantly. I wouldn't wish my life on anyone, except certain girls at school in my class and year, who I hated so much and who were the bullies.

Matthew was just eight years old, he was at the age of watching and giggling at children's television programmes.

We used to watch them together if Mother was out of the house either doing her cleaning duties at the school or if she had walked out on us. I felt I was regressing into a young child again and used the children's programmes as escapism from my real, cruel world. The worrying thing is that I actually enjoyed watching them and Matthew and I used to mimic cartoon voices. One of our favourite programmes was Animal Magic with Johnny Morris, we used to pretend to also talk to the animals in a clumsy, daft voice, just like Johnny Morris did. He was a brilliant presenter. We loved the animal programmes best, after all, compared to humans animals couldn't hurt us as much.

Blue Peter with John Noakes and his sheepdog called Shep was one of our other favourites, especially as Doreen kindly bought me Blue Peter annuals each year now for Christmas. I especially loved reading about the Blue Peter pets.

It seemed all our troubles were gone when we watched any animal television programmes. Matthew and I would laugh so much we had tears in our eyes about the antics of Rod Hull and Emu. Our other special programmes were Tales of the Riverbank, which involved real live animals such as Hammy Hamster and G.P. the guinea pig. These animals would be either rowing small boats, flying small aeroplanes or just running around the grass or falling into small puddles of water. I am sure there was a story to tell somewhere in all the chaos! But we loved it and thought it was hilarious.

Mentally, I suppose you could say I was a combination of 'regression and progression'. I did like adult comedy such as the Carry On films that were sometimes on a Sunday afternoon, and also another favourite Love Thy Neighbour, as it was just well written and so funny with the banter between neighbours and going to the local social club drinking. It reminded me of my nana and grandad in Hull, drinking at their local pub or club at the end of Newland Avenue. Unfortunately, my regression stage was later going to affect my future close relationships, where I was to be accused of being immature and childish. Well maybe I was immature at times, but this was MY escapism from my life of what seemed like being in a living hell.

It was also the year of Multi-Coloured Swap Shop with Noel Edmonds and Keith Chegwin. This was a Saturday morning children's programme on television that had music, guests and also you could phone in to swap your toys. Not that Matthew and I had any toys to swap but we enjoyed the programme anyway. One of the Saturday shows came from Hull City Football Ground (Boothferry Park as it was called then), it was live. As soon as we put the television on we saw Cheggers in Hull with a small crowd around him with amber and black football scarves. We nagged and nagged my father to take us to the Hull City Football Ground in the car, it was only about three or four miles from where we lived. 'Please take us in the car, Dad,' we begged, cried and asked politely. It was too far for us to walk in time, as the programme would have finished by the time we got there. My father was never impulsive or even excited. 'Pleeeeeaseeee ... we will never ask for anything else ever again,' we both begged. It was to no avail. He couldn't even be bothered to take us somewhere different on the spur of the moment. It wasn't even far away, we were both devastated. We had to watch others there at the football ground, whilst we had to stay at home, upset and watching from a distance. Of course back at school some of the lads were saying that they went to see Cheggers and the television crew were there and how exciting it was. I was still annoyed with my father. We didn't usually ask for anything, and now I knew why. Matthew and I were always disappointed. My motto now was, 'If you don't ask, you won't be disappointed.'

My Christmas presents from my parents seemed to be a bit more 'adult' this year, such as art straws – which to be honest you could not do a lot with except plait or weave the hollow paper straws into limited different shapes – and Plasticraft, which was a clear resin that you put in moulds along with small shells or glitter to make clear plastic jewellery or small displays. Another surprise gift was Flower Drops. This was to make your own pretend flowers. You had a thick wire as the flower stem, then fuse wire that you had to bend into shapes to make the petal design. Small tubs of acrylic paint came in the set and you dipped the petal shapes into the paint, for it to create a coloured petal. Unfortunately, once the wire and paints had been used up, that was it, very short-lived and I wasn't allowed any replacements. I must admit it was my favourite present.

At Hessle High School I was now sat next to Lorraine in Mrs Raymond's class. She was by nature a very quiet and nervous girl, but very talented with a good memory. The poor girl must have thought I was a whirlwind of craziness, but we got on well. She didn't have the same hobbies as me and wasn't talented in music or sports, in fact I think she hated them both! But she was very studious and intellectual and would go far in life. She knew things that I hadn't a clue about; she already knew about colour and light refraction, and she was also good at maths, unlike me! She invited me over to her house so we could go out on our bikes together. Lorraine lived near Boothferry Road in Hessle, which was easy to get to from my house on bike as the 'drains' had now been concreted over, making an easy shortcut through the long roads such as Richmond and Sunningdale Road.

I rode on my ladies' bike, which was still too big for me, to her house. We went into her bedroom where she showed me her main Christmas present from her parents of a gold ingot necklace. She said that although she could wear it, she was told by her father it was an investment for her. When she showed me it in her jewellery box, I kept holding it and feeling the weight and texture of the ingot, and feeling the chain, I had never handled actual gold before. It was amazing. She was so lucky to receive such a present for Christmas from her parents. I shouldn't be ungrateful, but my packet of paper art straws and Flower Drops seemed to pale into insignificance. No one had ever bought me any jewellery.

To the outside world everyone thought we were a typical family with '2.4 children', as they used to quote on the television. In reality I felt like Matthew and I just existed and never lived. Each day we were alive was a bonus as when Mother started hitting us with those thick sticks from the Flatley dryer. She didn't know when to stop. I had massive red scar marks on the back of my legs and Matthew had them across his back. My father used to have to pull or drag Mother off us as she just seemed to carry on hitting us faster and faster until we nearly passed out with the pain and from crying so loud. If he wasn't home (which was 99% of the time) then we still dreaded every step in the house in case we upset her. I knew there was no escape. But also now knew by visiting Lorraine's house that Matthew and I were treated unfairly and cruelly by our parents. Her parents would never treat her (or her younger sister that I had briefly met) in that way. They actually had respect for their daughters, and I admired them.

Besides being bullied for my music skills, I was also bullied for my love of sport and participation in gymnastics. I remember P.E. (physical education as it was called in those days) with a teacher called Mrs Lowther – who I instantly hated. She once set some coursework to write an essay on a famous sporting person and why you admire them. All the girls were choosing current famous people such as tennis players Bjorn Borg, Chris Evert and gymnasts like Olga Korbut and Nadia Comaneci. I knew I was too bulky to be a gymnast. My gymnastic skills had now waned slightly; my talent now was in body strength and weight training. Therefore, I chose Muhammad Ali (Cassius Marcellus Clay Jnr.) as my subject to write about, after all, he was famous as a boxer, extremely fit, talented and everything I now aspired to be. I could certainly use some of his talent to fight my mother off me – I could imagine her hitting me and me just turning round and with one punch knocking her over, or even killing her. God what a fantasy. I hoped that day would be soon. I was like a coiled spring from all the anger and aggression she had caused me, if she pushed me too far she would certainly get the brunt of my anger and I might explode. Then, of course she would blame me by saying she had already told people what a horrible child I was, and this just proved it.

I went to Hessle Library to borrow books about Muhammad Ali, his boxing and anything I could find with boxing in the title. I wrote pages and pages summarising his life story, how he aspired to be a boxer and any other interesting facts. I really got obsessed with his fame, the Olympics and also the racism he unfortunately had to endure.

For some reason we used to have written P.E. lessons in the girls changing rooms, sitting there with our exercise and text books on our knees trying to write. Mrs Lowther decided to mention about the famous people that had been written about by the other girls such as Bjorn Borg and Chris Evert, current tennis players and winners at Wimbledon. When it came to my essay, she was laughing, almost ridiculing me, and of course it made all the other girls laugh at me, even the bullies were laughing. I went bright red in the face and didn't say anything. Obviously she did not appreciate a good essay and also did not understand the work and effort I had put into this. She was another bitch and a bully. I hated her lessons. Suddenly I had a hating for sport. All my hobbies and interests now seemed to have disappeared from me, due to other people's interventions and now criticisms, and I felt defeated.

The class French teacher, Mrs Dalton, was a right stickler for punishment and even though we were in the top form, she used to give whole class detentions regularly. I think she took some sadistic enjoyment from this. I hated her also, and especially hated the French language, and had no interest in learning it. I wasn't ever going to go to France so why the hell should I learn the language? I was lucky to even travel the distance into Hull, so knew I would never get to France.

Mrs Dalton's detentions worked as follows – if someone (usually one of the lads) was disruptive in class then everyone got a detention. The idea, I think, was for that person to be bullied by the rest of the class, as I could not see any other reason to do this. Alternatively, if they did not own up to their disruptive behaviour, then everyone would still get a detention. Whichever rules she made up as she went along – it always ended up as a whole class detention. Or so she thought. The majority of the time I had to get back home to let Matthew in the house since Mother wasn't there – either at work or had left us, there was no way I was going to a detention and be even later home. After all I was caring for a child almost four years younger than myself!

Mrs Dalton had a weekly list of names of students who did not turn up for detention. There was obviously only me on it, as all the rest of the class were scared of her and had all attended, unless they were absent due to sickness. Compared to Mother she was the least of my worries. Mrs Dalton said she would put me on another detention – I still never attended. She was an obnoxious, old, grey-haired woman and I didn't even offer her my reasons for not attending as she had previously said that she wasn't interested in excuses. Little did she know it wasn't an excuse, it was a fact. If I didn't turn up at home then Matthew would be left either outside in the street, or alone in the house. I can honestly say I never went to any detention at that school as I did nothing wrong to warrant one. How can a school physically make you attend a detention? They can't, and they knew it.

The school thought they were clever, and sticking to their school policies, by sending letters to the house to advise my parents about me missing detention, and no doubt they also telephoned the house. They weren't clever enough to know that I would intercept the mail when it was delivered, and hide it in my bedroom, never to be seen again. I would destroy the letters, torn into shreds, in a public litter bin outside the shops on Gisburn Road. Shredding all the evidence – 'out of sight, out of mind', as I had been told by Mother!

If the school telephoned the house, or even the 'twagging officer' even called round about me missing detentions or missing school, there was no one there anyway. My father was always at work, and my mother had probably left again and gone to cry at her mother's house! If I was there, I certainly wouldn't be answering the door to anyone. My education suffered but I didn't care, I couldn't play my music anymore because of Mother not paying for my tuition and I now had no instrument, plus I hated sports now due to the cow bag P.E. teacher. I had actually thought about wanting to be a P.E. teacher or gym instructor at one time, but her attitude towards me certainly put me off.

Lessons at school were just frightening for me now. Our class, 1A1, had a teacher called Mr Sargieson for maths. He was nicknamed Sargy and was a notorious bully that also seemed to take some sadistic pleasure by shouting at individual students (including myself) or the whole class; he wasn't bothered as long as he got his loud voice heard. I hated maths at junior school, and definitely hated maths even more at secondary school. I actually had a mental block if I had to try and work out any mathematical equation in his lessons. To this day I hate this subject and he certainly didn't help my confidence. In fact he made it worse, and made me terrified of maths in general. He was another reason not to go to school.

Most of the time, on the occasions when Mother walked out on us, I used to see Matthew off to school in the morning. I would then just laze about the house with the dog. After all, why should I go to school? There were no positive reasons to attend school anymore. However, there were plenty of reasons NOT to go to school.

Why should I go to school for other children to bully and make fun of me and my War on Want uniform and white socks; be bullied for being good at music and sport; be shouted at by Sargy for not understanding maths, or even laughed at by Fowler for writing a good essay in P.E., to receive a detention on behalf of someone else who had done something wrong in class and I hadn't?! That was my logic, I was sticking to it as it was the truth! Why would anyone put themselves through that torture every day at school? What would I gain from attending school? Absolutely nothing – only more accusations, bullying and stress. I didn't even care if I left without any qualifications, my sanity was more important.

With Mother walking out on us erratically I didn't really know what to do – cry or laugh and be happy? I didn't know when she would be back and what mood she would be in when she eventually did come back. I was scared as well as relieved, but also emotionally upset with myself and didn't know if this was normal. I got used to walking on tiptoes in the house to be really quiet in case the neighbours heard, after all Doreen was at work, but her mother was in the house all day, and I was scared in case she heard me and told Doreen.

When Matthew came back from school at about 4pm, I would pour him a glass of milk as Mother didn't cancel the milkman so at least we got milk each day (except Sunday). I didn't know when he would get paid though. When the milkman came knocking on the door on a Saturday morning for his milk money, and if my dad was at work, we would just hide in our bedrooms. However, on the occasions Mother had left us, I did know how to cash in the family allowance. Mother kept the family allowance book in the coat cupboard under the stairs on a shelf, but the money from that didn't go very far. In those days anyone who had the allowance book could go into a post office and cash the weekly (or fortnightly) allowance, so we had a bit of money. This beige coloured book had pages inside, like vouchers, that were perforated, stamped and torn off at the post office by the cashier, in exchange for cash. I knew to buy staple things such as cornflakes, bread, butter, jam, Blue Ribbon biscuits (our favourites), cheap plain biscuits, packet custard, fruit, toilet rolls, dog food and orange juice for Matthew, and that was about it. I certainly wasn't going to buy any food that needed heating up on the gas stove or cooking in the oven, as fire still frightened me. I really wished we had an electric cooker like my grandma had, then I could buy some cans of food and warm up some baked beans or even soup.

Once I even treated myself to a 'mum' roll on anti-perspirant/deodorant from Grandways, as my mother wouldn't buy one for me, and just gave me a really old broken glass bottle of dried-up deodorant from the medicine cupboard in the kitchen, that I had to dip my fingers into and spread the dried-up gel-like liquid under my armpits. I think it was supposed to have a 'roller' on the top of it, but it had broken off. Yeah, she'd love it if I started to smell of body odour at school, especially in that heavy old-fashioned school blazer, and then I would be bullied for that also.

The family allowance money had nearly gone. For food I was limited to just boiling the electric kettle to make packet custard from powder and adding tinned fruit. I got on with it as no one would see us until about 8pm when my father would return from work and tell us again that he had meals from the post office canteen – oh well, that was okay then, don't worry about your children who were hungry and living off packet custard and cornflakes. He did not have a clue how to provide for his children and it showed. He should have stepped up to the mark and asked for some help, even from Doreen next door, but he never did. He also should have divorced Mother for the way she treated us, walking out on us randomly, but he didn't have the balls to do so. That made me resent him so much. I definitely wasn't bothered anymore about school, as no one took any interest, and not even my father had the time or patience to speak to me. Except when he kept telling me I had to 'run the house', meaning look after Matthew, do the cleaning, cooking, washing, shopping etc., all what Mother did. I think he forgot I was only twelve and I was supposed to attend school!

I learned to improvise with food. I created biscuit sandwiches (two Rich Tea biscuits held together with butter), and also an apple sandwich, a thinly sliced apple (left over in the fruit bowl) in between two slices of buttered bread – take it from me, it is revolting, and I had to reluctantly throw it outside onto the bird table. There wasn't a great deal I could improvise with anymore in the kitchen cupboards. I used some of the family allowance money to pay for Matthew's school dinners so at least he had something to eat during the day, whereas I went without, but it was a small sacrifice. I had the dog to feed also. Cheeky was used to having Pedigree Chum, well he soon changed to having the cheaper variety when I was around! He never went without though, and I even took him for extra walks after school hours and gave him extra dog biscuits. It wasn't his fault he had almost been abandoned by Mother, who had originally bought him. We all knew how he felt!

A bonus of my mother not being there that compensated for the hunger was that we weren't subjected to being slapped or hit by hand, slipper or a Flatley stick, and we wouldn't be mentally tortured. This was a massive benefit and relief as I knew I wouldn't have to sleep in my bed with one eye open at night, awaiting the punishment of being beaten for no apparent reason. I actually got some quality sleep when she wasn't there, only Matthew would wake me up by crying or needing something in the night like a glass of water – in the grand scheme of things, I could cope with that.

A few months later, when everything was almost back to normal at home and Mother had randomly returned, I remember going to see my aunty and cousin, Carol. They had moved out of my grandma's house a few years previously. They now lived in a terrace house with two bedrooms that had been converted into three, with the large front bedroom split into two for her and her brother. When I entered Carol's small bedroom I was amazed at how nice it looked compared to mine. With Carol being a bit younger than myself and still more 'girly', she was into Holly Hobbie. Her bedroom walls were covered in Holly Hobbie pink wallpaper, with images of

Holly Hobbie (who was an old-fashioned looking doll) and matching coloured hexagon shapes on the wallpaper. She also had a Holly Hobbie diary and some pictures up on the wall to match. It did look really smart. I can't remember if she had the bedding to match – knowing Carol, she probably did! I admit it wasn't my style but it did look fantastic. This gave me an idea to ask my mother if I could decorate my bedroom, obviously not with Holly Hobbie, but in a grown-up matching style I really liked.

I should have known better than to even ask Mother about this. The answer I got was 'It's my house, my rules. I do what I want in my house, if you don't like it just go ...' the verbal outburst went on and on like a bloody broken record. I only asked if I could have some different wallpaper or paint the walls. She accused me of being ungrateful again. I was twelve years old, I had no say in the way she decorated my bedroom to suit herself. The woodchip wallpaper was painted lilac, along with the homemade wooden wardrobe and chest of drawers, I had old-fashioned flowery, with lace trim, curtains that would have suited an eighty-year-old woman, along with the ripped cheap, thin, pink, frilly and flowery eider-down. I hated pink and I hated flowery patterns. I had turned a blind eye to this originally as I knew not to argue, but seeing Carol's bedroom was a revelation, and although I wasn't jealous of her, I was jealous of the way she could have some input into how her own room could look. I didn't have that choice. I was counting down the years until I could leave home (four years' time) and finally have some say in how I could live and my surroundings. My flowery curtains stayed there until I left home years later. Mother was welcome to them, I would rather not have any curtains up at all than have those granny curtains anyway.

Carol and I became a bit closer as we became older, almost

like sisters. I enjoyed going to her mother's house as Carol and I had free rein of almost everything. We were hardly told off and we just talked and tidied up in the house. I didn't mind tidying up and dusting in her house as it was appreciated and was actually something constructive to do, we would do the housework and chat together. Plus my aunty made fabulous massive meals, and I could have extra portions if I wanted. It was a good deal.

We used to laugh if I was there on a Sunday. Her step-dad (who she treated as her real father) used to go to the local pub with his friend down the road, and then come back mid-afternoon after a couple of pints. I am sure he had a few more, but who cares! They had a massive radiogram in the back room. It looked a bit like a wooden sideboard, and when you lifted up the lid it separated into different compartments for playing the radio and also playing your records on a turntable. There was a compartment for storing your vinyl singles and albums also, and built-in wooden speakers.

Carol's father would say to her 'Put on some Fats for me', so she would oblige put on his favourite Fats Domino album on the radiogram and play it. We would all sing along or hum along if we didn't know the words (I certainly didn't know the words!). Her mum would even pretend dance and sing to the music as she also did the housework or finished cooking the dinner. It really tickled me, as to how a household could be so relaxed and friendly. After a few tracks of Fats, we had to put different records on, usually her father would ask for Jerry Lee Lewis or Bill Hailey and the Comets, whilst her mother would say 'No, no we want Elvis'. They all loved the 1960s and early 1970s music, and even though I didn't know much about this kind of music, I could see the attraction of it: it was lively and got people dancing and singing.

Back home was a different story, almost a different world.

Yes, we had a more modern radiogram, with metal legs, a black and metal unit with a clear plastic lid, but the albums we had were not quite the same. My father was still into his steam trains. He used to go to second-hand record shops either in Hepworth's Arcade in Hull, or at Cleveland's Records down Hessle Road and buy train albums. One album cover showed a black and white picture a steam train and a location. As my father played the album, full blast, we would get a running commentary from him that usually went as follows: 'Can you hear the birds in the trees? Can you hear the steam train approaching? Here it is coming slowly into the station. Can you hear the platform announcement? Can you hear the train whistle sounding? The birds are flying away now as they are frightened. Listen to the sound of that train, you can hear the steam and the brakes.'

For God's sake, it sounded like Ivor the Engine. In fact, no, Ivor was a lot more entertaining and a cartoon. Why the hell anyone would want to even buy such an album was beyond me – it could have been any train, at any place, just recorded by anyone. When he played it, the sound was deafening and vibrated in the room, as if the train was actually coming through the house, I felt sorry for the neighbours having to endure that noise. But if someone took enjoyment from it, who am I to criticise? The other albums in my father's collection involved bagpipes and drum bands. As much as I enjoy musical talent and bands, this drove me into a melt-down, the high-pitched noise of bagpipes were enough to put even the local dogs into a howling frenzy. It gave me bloody headache. At Christmas time we had the privilege of him playing his favourite Christmas album – in German. I think I knew all the words to Stille Nacht in German at the time.

My father thought he was being clever with his German

version albums. We just wanted normal music like the Top of the Pops albums with a picture of a random scantily clad, suggestive woman on the front cover! My father's music was what I would probably listen to if I wanted to commit suicide. My musical taste had changed and I felt supressed by my mother and father. I would have appreciated classical music if they had any, I had learned a lot at school, especially Vivaldi and the Four Seasons. I loved 'Summer', or even Elgar and the Enigma Variations, I think I had played some of that in the school orchestra in the past. It was beyond my parent's knowledge or understanding and I was frustrated. I could easily have smashed up all my father's albums in a rage of frustration, but had to refrain myself! It was bloody hard to do.

The only enjoyment I got was listening to the top forty on my small, blue, tiny portable radio that my aunty had bought me. I would listen to the Hit Parade on Radio One on a Sunday night between 5pm and 7pm in my lilac bedroom and wish I was many miles away.

CHAPTER 17

Disrespected and Dejected

The year was 1978 and I was fourteen years old. I could write the full book about this holiday, which is another one never to be forgotten. I've certainly never forgotten the trauma of these seven days of my life. The words 'family holiday' to most families mean that they will have adventures, sightseeing trips or a relaxing time, unfortunately nothing like that happened when my mother and family were involved. My good friend, Julie, used to go on family holidays to Wales that took hours to get there, but she always came back excited and had a good time. I didn't know that feeling.

This saga was initiated when my father came home from work at the post office one night, announcing that he had seen an advert for a caravan for hire for a week's holiday in a small village named Pateley Bridge (Near Harrogate, North Yorkshire). He said he wouldn't mind us going there on holiday in August instead of the usual holiday to the caravan at Hornsea. My mother wasn't happy, until he said that he would pay for it all himself. He had seen a hand written postcard pinned up on the staff noticeboard at work, advertising a caravan to let over summer, and thought it sounded like a good countryside break in a large static caravan. I couldn't blame him. I knew he hated Hornsea so much as that was where he was evacuated to during the Second World War. He used to tell us about his 'Aunty Ivy' who lived in a white cottage near Hornsea Mere. She looked after him and his brother when they were evacuees at the end of the war, she wasn't his real aunty, but she let him call her aunty.

When my father drove us to Hornsea to take us to the caravan, he sometimes used to call in and see his Aunty Ivy, much to my mother's disgust (or probably jealousy!). He did like his aunty and respected her for looking after him. But I think he missed his own mother during that time, so I think Hornsea brought back some bad memories of being apart from family. Mind you, compared to living in Hull a few miles from the city centre during the war, unsafe and bombed by the Germans numerous times, Hornsea must have seemed like a dream. It was a quieter, more relaxed place and not full of the usual hustle of bustle of the Newland Avenue area in Hull. With this in mind, my father wanted to get away from it all and into the countryside on holiday, so thought that Pateley Bridge sounded idyllic.

He seemed to forget that he now only had a Reliant Regal van (a three-wheeler), the same as on 'Only Fools and Horses', that had been converted into a so-called 'car', only by adding two very small back windows and a back seat that resembled a shelf. It wasn't yellow like Del Boy's but it was a dark metallic green colour. This van was bought off a neighbour who lived opposite (Alison's father), and seemed like a bargain to my father, as the cost of the car tax apparently was the same as a motorbike, so a lot cheaper than a normal car. The fact is that when Matthew and I travelled in it, sitting on the padded 'shelf' otherwise called a seat, our heads banged on the ceiling of the van as we were both tall. It only had a fibre glass shell, so we were literally bashing the top of our heads on rough fibre glass.

My father had also forgotten that the road to Pateley Bridge was very hilly compared to Hessle, Hull and Hornsea, and the car would have difficulty going up the hills. Also there was the conundrum of how he would fit us all in it, plus the dog, luggage and all bedding etc. Usually there would be an argument between Matthew and myself as we were squashed together in the back seat, which wasn't exactly large, in fact it was a good job we were so slim otherwise we'd have no chance of getting on that seat. We also usually felt travel sick in the back as we were being thrown around when the van went round corners, almost on one wheel. It was like being on a ride at Hull Fair. I can't even remember there even being seatbelts in the back as it was officially still a van, but what was vehicle safety in those days? Shove your children in the back of a car or van, and hope for the best!

So when the holiday travel day in August arrived, it was decided by my mother that my father, Matthew and the dog, plus luggage etc. would travel in the van to Harrogate, then they would meet us at the train station, so we could all go to Pateley Bridge. Mother and I had to go on the train to Harrogate. I was dreading it. I remember travelling from Hull train station and having to change trains at Leeds, I think, then transfer to Harrogate. My mother hadn't a clue where to go. I just followed like a shadow and daren't even speak. I remember feeling crap as I had started my periods that day and had a lack of resources, shall we say. Still, that was nothing new and I had no pocket money left to buy any towels, but I was used to that also and just used folded up loo roll. I soon learned how to improvise. Mother had started to give me a packet of ten towels per month, but that had dwindled off, plus it was never enough, ten towels wouldn't last me three days, never mind the seven days bleeding I had to endure. I felt uncomfortable all the time as I was forced to wear a flowery skirt, and was scared in case I leaked. By the time we arrived at Harrogate I was fraught and needed the loo, and my mother couldn't even find her way out of the train station, so that was a great start and we hadn't even begun the holiday.

We met my father, Matthew and the dog outside the train station, and all got in the van to travel to the caravan. They had already unloaded all the luggage and bedding etc. at the caravan, so there was room for us all. We travelled up hill and down dale and the van struggled, after all the engine size was only the cc of a motorbike, probably 600cc at the most. I remember the van struggling to get over a bridge over a river, and feeling sick in case we came off the road and fell over the side into the water.

Eventually, after about half an hour of driving at a slow, struggling pace, we made it to a small farmhouse in the middle of nowhere. I remember there was a small stream parallel to the road and my father saying 'Oh that is where we will get our fresh water.' Other than that quick statement, he was quiet so I knew something was wrong. We stopped the van and yes, there was a caravan at the side of a field near a farmhouse in a place named Glasshouses. It was like something from the 'Likely Lads' film, a small four berth tourer at the side of a field, that would be lucky to even move off the field in one piece. I reckon it hadn't been moved since it was first bought. So much for the large family static caravan full of mod-cons! The cost of the holiday would probably be the cost of the caravan to buy it! I could tell my father was embarrassed and waiting for my mother to say something, but what can you do when he'd made the effort to provide us a different family holiday he thought would be better than Hornsea? The caravan here also had no toilet or shower facilities.

The moody old woman at the farmhouse whose caravan it was said we could use an outside toilet situated in a veranda alongside the farmhouse, it had an old hand basin and that was it, only cold water and no hot water and certainly no bath or shower. I thought that this was the same as the caravan at Hornsea, he may as well have saved his money. I was hoping for a nice warm shower (that we didn't have at home). The outside loo was freezing and the cold wind blowing under the door didn't help, and that was in summer! I was wondering how I was going to survive this week of hell in a caravan that was the size of a shed and half the size of the caravan at Hornsea.

The night-time arrangements were horrendous. I had a small bunk bed at the bottom, and Matthew had a put-me-up nylon material hammock (that was supposed to be an upper bunk bed) above my small sleeping area. It was claustrophobic and Matthew's body and backside was almost touching mine! I kept poking him on his back just to annoy him so he'd shout out.

That first night I was bursting for a wee and knew I needed to go to loo because of my heavy women's problems! Everyone was getting ready for bed and I said 'I'm just popping to the loo.' Well that was it, Mother wouldn't let me go out 'You've just been!' she stated harshly at me. I said I desperately needed to go. So I was even banned from going for a wee, I was busting and also knew if I didn't get to the loo, I would have a mishap with my period problems. I hated her. How dare she stop me going to the loo? My father was weak and didn't stick up for me. I ended up not sleeping at all as I needed to go to the loo, had stomach pain, and didn't want to wet the bunk bed. I suffered stomach pains all night.

Mother got her comeuppance the next morning as I had 'leaked' with my period all over the sheets, bedding and my nightdress (I wasn't allowed to wear pyjamas). I got out of the bunk where I slept and I was literally blathered in it. Mother went mad and told father, I shouted that I TOLD her I needed to go to the toilet last night and she had stopped me. She said I wasn't normal and that no normal person would leak that much – well later on in life I found I had endometriosis and fibroids, so that explained it, not that she cared. She was on the rampage and managed to find a black bin bag and put the sheets and my nightdress in it and announced to my father that he would drive us to Harrogate to a launderette. He was huffing and puffing also, as it was his first holiday and he wanted to go elsewhere to see some steam trains. I couldn't bloody well win. I got no sympathy about me feeling crap, or even given any more sanitary towels. I felt I was just keeping my head above water, is this what normal families did? I didn't know. I needed to get a shower but there was no shower or bath, only one sink with cold water in the farmhouse outbuilding. I was losing the will to live, but didn't show any emotion as that is what she wanted.

We all got into the van with the bin bag of bedding and my father drove the van to Harrogate to try and find a launderette. I remember going into a launderette and thinking that at least it was warm and clean. So we stayed there probably about one hour, then put the clean laundry into the van, and my father parked up somewhere else so we could walk around the shops or go sightseeing. Then Mother suddenly started picking on me, saying my hair was like rats' tails. I said it was like rats' tails (as she called it) as I hadn't washed it for two days as she hadn't bought any shampoo with her and also the water was freezing cold in the sink so it would never get clean as I needed warm water. At home I sometimes used talcum powder as 'dry shampoo' in between washes, but that only lasted a few hours, she always stopped me washing my hair and to this day I do not know why. I had grown my hair to shoulder length and quite liked it, she was jealous of it. She had always had short hair with a poodle perm. She asked my father what he thought and he said that we needed warm water really to get it clean – I think he was being diplomatic and trying to calm her down. I knew she was building up to her revenge for me accidentally soiling the sheets through no fault of my own.

The next thing I know, I am literally being dragged by my shoulders into a random barber's shop in Harrogate with other men and boys, having haircuts. She demands that someone cuts my hair and announces to everyone that it is a disgrace and looks like rats' tails. Yeah, thank you, Mother, telling the whole shop full of customers that are now looking at me. I said nothing. It wasn't even worth arguing and wasting my breath. I then had what you could call a sort of 'basin cut' on my hair. Mother was sat watching all the time, seeing if I had a reaction. I made sure I didn't react, just to annoy her, even though I felt like crying inside and I think I may have shed one tear but made out it was a bit of hair in my eye. She just kept telling the woman cutting my hair that my hair was a disgrace, as if I wasn't there. I was so embarrassed in front of all these strangers.

When I came out of the barber's shop my father was sat outside on a wall. I could tell he was not impressed at all, but he made out the basin cut suited me. My confusion was that they had cut it, but not washed it anyway, so it was just shorter rats' tails then, so what was the point in that? The only point was to make me feel inferior and her superior, to show me who would always be the boss. It was like I had a boy's hair cut on a round girl's face. Matthew, of course, thought it was hilarious and could not stop pointing and laughing at me. I would have done the same to him, so could not really say anything.

I just wanted to be alone but had to act like I was fine and loved my new boy's hairstyle, short and basin like. I remember walking around Harrogate in a daze and just walking for the sake of it. I hated walking anyway as it gets you nowhere at a slow pace, I'd rather put on my white trainers and run.

Oh and at least that night, back in the small caravan, Mother let me go to toilet at the end of the day, she seemed to learn from her mistake the previous night.

As the week rolled on Matthew and I became more and more bored. One day we had to visit the Bronte museum. I am not into history. I am a person who tries to look forward and not back, so visiting a fusty old house did not really impress me. It was even older than my grandma's or nana's houses! Mother made out it was fantastic. Well take it from me, she was lucky to even understand the Hull Daily Mail (our local paper), never mind books written by the Bronte sisters. Even at school Wuthering Heights or Jane Eyre didn't astound me. I didn't really understand the plot, and I'm sure you could have written the book in about a quarter of the pages. But that's just my opinion as a teenager; I preferred modern autobiographies and true facts books. So this was a long, tedious boring day out for Matthew and me. I had never been so bored in all my life, I felt I was in a trance-like state.

During the week I also remember one day my father spotting a sign for Stump Cross Caverns when he was driving, and it was nearby. Well, that sounded superb, I thought, underground caverns and exploring. It could be like a Secret Seven book! We got there after a bumpy ride in the van, parked up, and Matthew and I were already running from the van to the entrance to have a look. We didn't realise it was quite a way underground – even better, we could not wait. My father paid for us all to go into these underground caves or caverns. It was very dark but there were some lights near the corner of the caves and also on the many steps down. It was quite claustrophobic, but I loved it and Matthew was trotting down the steps at his own pace. We then turned round to see Mother and Father arguing. Apparently she felt claustrophobic and couldn't go down the steps any further. My father was annoyed as he had paid for her and she seemed to want him to come back with her, which would mean that we ALL had to go back up the steps and leave. He refused, and let her return back to the main reception area, then caught up and carried on with us.

We had an amazing time, especially without Mother, who was a mix of a drama queen and bordering on bipolar at the best of times. My father even laughed about how to remember the difference between stalactites and stalagmites, you know the usual joke of 'tights come down', he was a different person when she wasn't there. I think he knew she treated us badly but felt his life would not be worth living if he disagreed with her. He knew he was in for some backlash as it was, when he surfaced from the caverns. How I wished he could be like a proper father to us and join in with us, not having to agree with Mother all the time. I knew that they would never divorce, so he had 'made his bed, so had better lie in it', so to speak, unfortunately, for the rest of his life.

When we eventually surfaced from the caverns, Mother was there with a face of thunder when we were all laughing about our experience. She said she felt ill and needed to go back to the caravan. Yeah, dramas again, spoiling our fun.

One day on the holiday we even ventured to Brimham Rocks, which Matthew and I enjoyed. We were running and climbing up the rocks and father was taking our photos. Mother was annoyed as she could not climb the rocks, she was lucky to even climb the stairs at home. She had the dog with her and was getting angrier, so I took the dog – he was only a small Yorkshire Terrier, so light as a feather, and carried him up the rocks also. I remember there is a photo of Matthew, Cheeky and me on the top of one of the rocks. I loved that photo as it seemed to show us at our happiest, somewhere that Mother couldn't reach and touch us, and with our dog that Matthew and I loved so much. It was our 'safe place': somewhere she couldn't hurt us. I wished I could have stayed up there forever.

CPSIA information can be obtained
at www.ICGtesting.com
Printed in the USA
LVHW031045290321
682805LV00001B/116